Commendations

This is a book which looks honestly at the impact of death on the writer and her family. She looks at the importance of childhood grief, and how things go wrong when a child is unable to grieve for a parent. Subsequent deaths have a profound effect and cause the writer to revisit her childhood loss.

As she experiences the tragic loss of her baby, followed by her father's death and then a teenage family friend, I felt great sadness, but also amazement that the human spirit can cope with so much loss. Then she is able to deal with her aunt's old-age and preparation for death in an amazing and healthy way.

This is a book which is written honestly and helps the reader understand the nature of bereavement. She looks at the struggles of trusting God during the dark times and the tension that causes.

Her lists of what helped and didn't help could be of help to others who want to care for those who are bereaved. The writer uses 'the comfort she has received to comfort others,' and continues to work and support those who are grieving.

What a journey of faith, endurance and hope!

Mary Dicker CSS Dip CPC,
Trainer, Supervisor and Counsellor,
Fegans Child and Family Care.

*Time to say Goodbye – a deeply evocative title for
a deeply moving and personal story. I've known
Barbara since we were 7-year-old best friends. In
this book I see that she has come on a long and
often painful journey of both self-discovery, and the
discovery of a growing relationship with God.*

*Today, death and grief are among the most
difficult subjects to talk about. Barbara does
so with a rare honesty and clarity, that is both
poignant and raw. She gives expression to our own
often unspoken thoughts and feelings, and her
words bring comfort and insight.*

*This is not the grey little girl I once knew;
Barbara, the author, and the woman, has found
"the colour in her voice". Thank-you Barbara.*

Jackie Cooke
Lifelong friend and former social worker
and speech and language therapist

*Barbara writes movingly and with a touching
honesty about death: her mother, two children, a
faithful father and a beloved aunt. She has learnt
many lessons and her desire to reflect back all she
has learnt will I am sure bring wisdom, strength
and above all faith into the lives of many of us
facing or living with bereavement. The heart of this
book reveals One who ultimately has the power
to bring peace and healing into the devastation
of loss."*

Steve Clifford, General Director,
Evangelical Alliance

*In her book Barbara Pymm takes us into her
most personal experiences of bereavement and
grief in the belief and hope that what she has
been through will be a help and encouragement*

to those who are facing similar challenges. Her vulnerability is touching and the honesty with which she shares failures and victories from the details kept in her journals, will provide a mirror for some who will identify and recognise themselves and so find the joy and freedom which Barbara now enjoys.

John Noble
Author, speaker and Chairperson of The National Charismatic Leaders Conference 1984 – 2007

This moving story will resonate with many people wanting to find a positive way to make sense of the prison imposed by suffocating raw grief. It also shows how a church community can provide such comfort and warmth in times of tragedy. Finally it reminds us that when we feel most isolated and lost in grief – our hunger to belong is nourished by beliefs that bring both peace and hope.

Julie Stokes OBE
Consultant Clinical Psychologist & Founder of Winston's Wish – charity for bereaved children

This is a rare glimpse into the vacuum and pain experienced through loss. This publication could be a source of comfort, strength and hope.

Gerald and Anona Coates – Speakers/Authors

The death of a loved one is never easy. This book will help bereaved adults by enabling them to understand their feelings and allow themselves to grieve. It will also help those in supporting roles.

Anne Davies,
Founder of Jigsaw4u, charity for bereaved children

*Time to Say Goodbye triggered a few tears
as I was reading it...grief is common to us all.
Barbara writes movingly from the heart about her
experiences of loss and, at the same time, offers
practical insights into how to let the pain of grief
pass through unhindered. With pain avoidance
being one of the driving forces in society, this
book will enable anyone to engage with grief
meaningfully and find hope, faith and courage on
the journey.*

*Caroline Kennedy,
Leader of Pioneer Network of Churches*

Time to Say Goodbye

Steps in learning to grieve

Barbara Pymm

RoperPenberthy Publishing Ltd

Published by RoperPenberthy Publishing Ltd,
Springfield House,
23 OatlandsDrive,
Weybridge,
Surrey
KT13 9LZ

ISBN 978-1-903905-73-9

Typeset by **documen**, www.documen.co.uk
Printed in the United Kingdom by Knowledgepoint, Reading

Contents

Acknowledgements

I'm so grateful, God, for all you've done in my life. Without you there would have been nothing to write about. You've led me on this journey and shone your light on my path and given me hope when I would have despaired. And in the telling of my story, so many times I've asked you to bring to the page the insightful image, the expressive phrase or the fitting word. The best of this book I owe to your inspiration.

Thank you Alison for befriending me at college when we met as fellow students at the College of Sarum St Michael in Salisbury. You have an amazing gift of encouragement. You believed in me. When I had buried myself in my emotional pain you drew me out. Thank you for understanding me so well and giving me the confidence to find myself. Thank you too for your current input – your perceptive appreciation of my poetry/reflections, encouraging me in my selection for the appendix and reassuring me in my choice of words.

Thank you Cobham Christian Fellowship (and later Pioneer People and Pioneer Engage) for showing me God's love and acceptance and for creating a loving family where I could belong. You gave me a safe place to go even deeper. Thank you friends for your courage in expressing your love for us when Michael died. Thank you friends who shared the pain of your miscarriages. Thank you for your vulnerability. All my friends who have loved me and supported me on my journey, whether still walking with me or on a different path … thank you so much.

Thank you Malcolm and my family – Jonathan, Rachel, Catherine and Lizzy. You've shaped me and given me a reason for living when I might have got entangled in myself. You've been positive and encouraged me when I've felt weak and weary. Thank you Malcolm for helping me create the footprint bullet points! Thank you, Jonathan, for reliving that traumatic evening when you were not quite 7 and your baby brother died. Thank you too for sharing your memories and reflections of the time 7 years later when your best friend, Matthew, died. Thank you Rachel, Catherine and Lizzy for enthusing with me at the completion of this project.

Thank you Tim and Jill, Hannah and Naomi for the privilege of including me in your grief for Matthew. Thank you for allowing me to explore with you your precious memories and how Matthew's life and death had impacted each of you so deeply. Thank you for sharing the details of your story which brought healing to me and released grief for my mum that had been suppressed for so many years.

Thank you Richard (my brother) for writing to me when I needed to delve into the facts surrounding Mum's death and for being willing to share your letter so publicly. Thank you too for reminding me of details of Dad's life and for contributing your own grief and memories. Thank you too for alerting me to substantives and bringing grammatical order to my chapter ends! Thank you, Miriam (my sister in law) and Peter Groat (her father) for your comments and support, drawing from me a fuller portrayal of Dad.

Thank you Liz Ray for your idea that I 'simply tell my story' when I might have bombarded readers with what I had learnt! Thank you Anne Davies, founder of Jigsaw4u, for encouraging the book in its very early stages and ingeniously recommending the 'what helped' and 'what could help' at the close of each chapter. Together, Liz and Anne, your comments brought the balance of narrative and helpful suggestions for which I'd been searching.

Thank you Chris Leonard for your practical advice on getting a book written and published. You got me started and you redirected me when I was in danger of going off track. And it was you who pointed me towards Cruse.

Thank you Cruse for your comprehensive training which verified so much that I sensed intuitively about grief. Thank you Jigsaw4u for your therapeutic activities and the balloon release that set *me* free. Thank you Cruse and Jigsaw colleagues who cared for my emotional wholeness.

Thank you, Jamie Wright, for reading early versions and for recommending that I have an introduction to set out my purpose in writing. Sometimes you challenged my use of a particular word or the inclusion of irrelevant details. I appreciated your thoughtful criticism. Other times you valued and celebrated the outcome and I felt elated.

I can't thank you enough, Jackie Cooke, for reading the whole book at least four times and some chapters many times more. Thank you for reading it chapter by chapter at least twice. Thank you for kindly reading it all through again to be faithful and conscientious in your commendation. And, finally, thank you for painstakingly scrutinising it yet again with a fine toothcomb looking for typos and even spotting spaces that had mysteriously appeared on your computer!

Most of all, Jackie, thank you for following in my footsteps of grief. I've been touched by your tears. I've been uplifted by your insightful comments. Most of all I've felt understood. You penetrated the very heart of the book. As my lifelong friend from the age of seven you knew me then and you know me now and you can verify that I'm not who I once was. You can confirm that I've learnt to say goodbye!

Treasures of Darkness

I will give you the treasures of darkness, riches stored in
secret places, so that you may know that I am the LORD...

(Isaiah 45:3)

The Spirit of the Sovereign LORD is on me,
because the LORD has anointed me ...
He has sent me to bind up the broken-hearted,
to proclaim freedom for the captives
and release from darkness for the prisoners,
²to proclaim the year of the LORD's favour ...
to comfort all who mourn,
³and provide for those who grieve in Zion—
to bestow on them a crown of beauty
instead of ashes,
the oil of gladness
instead of mourning,
and a garment of praise
instead of a spirit of despair.

(Isaiah 61:1-11)

Praise be to the God and Father of our Lord Jesus Christ,
the Father of compassion and the God of all comfort, who
comforts us in all our troubles, so that we can comfort those
in any trouble with the comfort we ourselves have received
from God.

(2 Cor 1:3-4)

What Treasure I have Found!

The peace of One who holds my hands in His and knows the path
*   I've travelled,*
Who knows the pain I've carried and the fears that have
*   tormented me*
And holds me tight.

The joy of One who laughs with me and frees me from my past,
Who knows me through and through
Yet loves me so completely.

The freedom of One whose healing lightness He can work in me,
As body yielded I express the fullness in my spirit
For all He's done for me.

The voice of One who whispers gentle words – accepting love,
Who comforts in my hurt,
Who challenges when I need stirring from passivity.

The majesty of One who always surprises me by being bigger
Than when I saw him last,
Who is beyond the tininess and compartmentalising of my mind.

What treasure I have found!

Introduction

What does it mean to say goodbye? Can I share with you the journey I've taken through my grief? This is a personal story, intimately told. But it's also a universal story.

Personal story is powerful. It was suggested that I simply tell my story and allow readers to absorb what they will. Sometimes people can't talk about their own grief but can engage with a story that's told, sometimes recognising themselves ... sometimes struck by how different their response has been.

I hope that my story may provide a language to articulate your feelings, perhaps describing thoughts you've barely acknowledged. I've tried to reflect honestly to give you opportunity to resonate with your own grief and find your way forward. Will you look at my steps and consider what might help you?

I was only eight when my mother died and I didn't know how to grieve. There was no goodbye. In fact there was little acknowledgement of any grieving process.

When my baby died I discovered ways to grieve that I found more helpful than others and this book began in embryo form. A following miscarriage left me mystified by the silence and lack of focus for grief. How we need to acknowledge it as bereavement and give space to mourn! In fact these first three bereavements together underlined for me the necessity of a goodbye.

My father's death was anticipated but I found that being 'prepared' for loss doesn't necessarily lessen its impact. When my son's best friend died I was more the bewildered onlooker wanting to alleviate suffering and confused by its huge effect on me. This bereavement challenged me to confront events that I hadn't faced with the death of my mum. It began a journey of healing to the grief that had been suppressed for many years.

My aunt had in part taken the place of my mother. So her death was another significant loss in my life. Yet I'd learnt so much. I was in a better place.

But there were still some deeper paths to walk. Both in speaking and in writing, others challenged me that I was withholding some emotion. Clearly there was more to be done.

My journey through grief was intertwined with a journey to faith. My relationship with God had grown significantly. Further steps of wanting to be more transparent with him created a desire to uncover these hidden emotions. I didn't always like what came to light. I found yet more healing through forgiveness and began to let go of the destructive behaviours that had become so intertwined with my personality and for which I needed to forgive myself.

I realise some readers may not share my faith. But apparently more people believe in God than don't. Certainly at a time of death people tend to think more about faith and an after-life. Some find in suffering and death a philosophical issue and wrestle with some of the conflicting thoughts and emotions underlying my own battles. But for those of no faith or of a different faith from the Christian one, there is plenty of practical help which would be equally applicable.

Involvement with bereavement organisations not only gave me the tools to help others but required me to reflect further on my own steps through grief. In order to become a Cruse counsellor for children as well as adults I participated in a training course by Fegans. This gave me the artistic opportunity to create a picture symbolising how I felt as a child of eight following the death of my mum.

I cut my figure from silver paper because I was a reflective girl – introspective and supersensitive to the reactions of others. Fearful of adding to my father's pain, I became trapped by my grief – unable to cry or to talk about what had happened. I represented this state with thick black bars – a prison from which I longed to escape! On the ground were many footprints where I'd slipped in the mud of self-blame, withdrawal and insecurity.

Outside –out of sight and out of reach – were coloured feathers. The varying colours represented the full expression of my emotions – a contrast to the monotony of my grey numbness. Feathers intimated the freedom to be found in the supernatural realm – hope in God. I placed them together to create a rainbow – a promise from God of release from my pain and my grief.

As I completed the prison I saw that it looked like a gate. Indeed it had swung open to set me free. The path of my life protruded beyond – to a world of acceptance, of friends and of laughter.

My footprints caught the light and I noticed they were gold. Could it be that even my slip-ups will one day be used by God for his glory? Could my faltering steps help others as I share my own journey of faith and forgiveness? Could they too be released from their prison into freedom?

In order to facilitate this process I've closed each chapter by picking out what helped and what didn't help. I've also included what could help for the reader or the griever, generalising from my own experience – both good and bad. I discovered things that helped and times where I missed the way. Those that were helpful I've indicated with a footprint bullet point. I trust these will be the footprints of my picture and, as light falls on them, they will be as gold.

Barbara Pymm
2012

1 *Mum*

I was eight years old. My mother was in hospital. She'd been ill for months but I didn't know why. One December morning my father, brother and I spelt out 'GET WELL SOON' with cards outside her window. Hospital rules prohibited children from visiting.

A few days later my aunt came up from Somerset to stay. She'd gone straight to the hospital and had still been there when I'd gone to bed. Next morning I got into bed with her. She stroked my hair gently, 'Mummy's gone to be with Jesus.'

The words were spoken tenderly, belying the enormity of this information. I lay there silently trying to make sense of this. Mum had gone to heaven. How could this be? I was expecting her to get well soon – just like the message we'd given her five days before. I didn't cry. It was too overwhelming. My world had fallen apart. What would happen now?

I voiced only one question, 'Can I live with you?'

It was a question sparked off by the events of the previous summer. In April my mum had explained gently that she had a little spot on her tummy and that she was going into hospital to have it sorted out. I was to stay with my aunt in Somerset. I'd protested incredulously, 'You don't go into hospital about a little spot!' But I soon realised she was serious.

'What about my school?' I exclaimed. We never took holidays in school time. But it had all been arranged. My mum's sister, my Aunty Ruby, was a headmistress of Hamp Infant school in Bridgwater in Somerset and I would go to the junior school on the same site.

And so I'd stayed with my aunt in Somerset for three months that summer while my mum was in hospital. I even had my eighth birthday there. I'd never been away from my family before – not even for one night! But Aunty Ruby was very kind. She lived with her friend, Joan, and it was a novelty for them to have a little girl to teach new card games and to help make cakes.

It had been a delightful time – long summer days with strawberry cream teas and trips to local swings and slides. I loved the Somerset countryside, welcoming the contrast from the London suburbs where I'd lived for the past five years – as long as I could remember. The Somerset fields were full of cowslips and other wild flowers. We went for walks where I'd find dream houses with thatched roofs. I imagined living in them one day with loads of cats and dogs.

School too was actually pleasurable. My school in Stoneleigh had been very pressured with Maths or English homework every night and weekly tests. Everything was geared to getting through the 11+. I didn't know there were any subjects other than Maths and English!

Suddenly I was transported to a school with wider horizons where we learnt dressmaking, gardening and writing poetry. Topic work was a fascinating new experience for me. I loved the freedom of taking my own notes from books. There was a wonderful climbing frame that we could use at playtimes and I learnt all sorts of skills and ways of swinging upside down. I was the new girl and everyone wanted to be my friend. This school was almost a holiday in itself.

Unfortunately my return to my old school had been less pleasant. It was July when my mum had been well enough to have me again. I arrived back at my old school just in time for the end of term tests. I was tested on everything – even the radio programmes I'd missed. I didn't do well. My teacher was very cross. 'Didn't you learn *anything* at your other school!' she exclaimed.'

I felt guilty, though not sure what I should have done differently – after all I hadn't devised the curriculum at my Somerset school! But it seemed I'd even forgotten things I'd known *before*. I'd been well into the top third of the class at Easter but now I was at the bottom, as she kept telling me. I felt very stupid and lost a lot of confidence. Even my friends seemed to have forgotten me. They had made other friends and it took time for me to fit in again. My idyllic experience with Aunty Ruby in Somerset had exacted a high price after all.

But the following month we'd been on holiday as a family. We *all,* including my mum, went to Jersey in mid August for two weeks – on an aeroplane! This was most exciting – a new experience for us all. Previous holidays had been by boat and train. We voted this holiday one of our best. It seemed we went to 'a different seaside every day'. We all swam. It was good to be together – to be a 'normal' family again.

But my mum got worse. Two months later she had to go back to hospital. Did I ask why? Was I told why? I don't remember being told anything. Her illness was shrouded in mystery.

For this hospital stay my parents judged it would be better for me to stay living at home. I'd found it so hard to settle back into my old school after being away in the summer. Now I had the same scary cross teacher for a second year. She was unlikely to make it any easier if I went away again. It was decided that we would have a resident housekeeper, so there would be someone in the house when I came back from school.

My father had been preoccupied with visiting my mother whenever possible – with a mask. Infection was always a danger. The visits hadn't included me – except that isolated occasion outside with the Lexicon cards. At the time I felt lonely and a little rejected. A gloomy cloud hung over the household that I sensed but couldn't articulate. I didn't enjoy having the housekeeper and the memories of my time in Somerset were still fresh in my mind – a time when I'd been happy and cared for.

So, with the news of my mother's death, it was natural to ask Aunty Ruby if I could go to live with her now. She replied that she would love to have me, but Daddy and my brother, Richard, would need me to stay with them and keep the family together. There didn't seem much else to say.

That very same morning I was taken to school. My father and aunt went in to tell my teacher. I stayed in the playground and told my best friend, Jackie. It seemed like everything was carrying on as usual. Would things still really be the same? What would it mean in my life? I felt dazed – numb – helpless. Later the class was told my news. One girl, not a close friend, bought me a box of mints. It was a nice thought, but I didn't want special treatment. I wanted to be like everyone else.

But from then on, I wasn't. Mums crop up in children's conversation all the time. It was a constant reminder that I was different. I was 'strange' – just like the meaning of my name 'Barbara' – strange, foreign. All my classmates had both parents – that was normal then as divorce was rare. I was the odd one out.

The funeral was the following Monday. I wasn't included – nor was my brother, Richard, at twelve – even though he'd asked to go. In those days children didn't attend funerals. Instead, Jackie's mum took Jackie and me to see Father Christmas. It was meant to be a treat but it didn't feel right. I felt shut out and excluded. Relatives from Sussex and Somerset were coming. Looking back I know I wanted to be part of the family occasion however sad. At the time I kept quiet.

Father Christmas gave me a plastic doll with no clothes – its limbs moulded to its body. I said, 'Thank you.' But what a contrast to my dolls at home with outfits lovingly made by Mum! One of my clearest memories of my mum is of her sitting at an old treadle sewing machine, making a dress for me. With every outfit she made me, either knitted or sewn, she would make a tiny version for my favourite doll. But this doll from Father Christmas was like me – trapped, naked – vulnerable.

My friend, Jackie, didn't like her present from Father Christmas and said so. I marvelled at her response. Had I tried for too long to be 'good' and to fit in? Things had happened to me that I was powerless to do anything about. Was I now accepting everything unquestioningly?

Looking back now I believe my spirit had been crushed – I was deeply wounded to the core of my being. The inner me was suffocated, swept aside. I had lost the strength to stand up – to express my wishes, my thoughts, my feelings. All were submerged in a sea of blackness. My identity had been defeated. I was vulnerable to every blow – unable to discern what I was free to challenge from what I was forced to accept. All strength of self had been obliterated.

At the time I simply reflected that Jackie and I were different. I observed that she talked more freely about what she liked and didn't like. I wondered if I'd ever been like that.

That Christmas my father gave me a doll with long hair like mine, dressed in a miniature version of my school uniform – apparently this was my mum's idea. How could my mum have planned such a special gift for me? This doll brought her closer. I loved this doll. I called her Jennifer and played schools with her constantly.

But something odd was happening in me. I found it impossible to talk about my mum. Apparently I'd tried to talk to my dad once, but he became 'upset' so I'd kept off the subject since. In our family we always tried not to 'upset' anyone. I'd always been responsive to the reactions of other people. Had I now become supersensitive?

Was I scared of my dad's intense emotion? I think I found feelings too dangerous and unpredictable. I didn't want to be stirring them up in other people any more than in myself. It was easier and less embarrassing for us both if I avoided talking about my mum.

Or was I taking my cue from my dad? The lack of information preceding my mum's death …the conspiracy of silence…had this contributed to a taboo area? Was I just fitting in with what I assumed were family expectations?

Was I putting a lid on all the emotions I was struggling with? Perhaps initially denial was helpful to escape an intolerable intensity of emotion. But I'd got stuck there. I knew clearly she had died but was my lack of verbalisation hindering my ability to process her death? In some way I believe it did. My grief was trapped inside.

Expressing sadness usually includes crying, shouting and screaming – our voices so powerfully communicate emotion. Perhaps talking is the least emotional function of the voice. But I couldn't even manage that. I didn't articulate my memories and I didn't voice my questions.

If I kept quiet, no one would know what I thought or felt. I could control things better and keep life more peaceful. Or so I thought. It was a futile attempt to control the pain. It seemed like an inner escape. I didn't know that in the process I was locking *myself* into a dungeon that was even more inaccessible to the outside world.

Whatever the reason, I clammed up ... for years and years. If Dad or Richard mentioned my mum I would listen, but I would never pursue the conversation.

So I didn't talk and I still hadn't cried. Instead I internalised my grief. At times I was conscious of a big lump of pain, knotting my stomach, weighing me down. Sometimes it stifled me leaving me breathless. Always there was an inner crying – a weight of misery locked within yet strangely leaving me feeling empty and alone.

The death of a mother has practical implications. From the time of my mum's final stay in hospital, we'd had the resident housekeeper to care for me. I didn't like this. What control a housekeeper could exert! Home was no longer a place of safety where I could be myself. I tried even harder to be 'good'. I retreated further inside myself. What delicious freedom when the housekeeper had a day off! I would run about the house released from the striving to be perfect.

I walked back from school one day and found the door locked. There was no sign of the housekeeper. I sat on the doorstep and waited for two hours till my father came back from work. We went in together and found she'd left. She'd gambled money given her for groceries and had left a string of unpaid bills.

I tried to hide my relief – clearly this was a nuisance for my father. But I hadn't felt comfortable with her. Her role included responsibility for me but there was nothing motherly about her. There'd been no relationship of caring or warmth.

Soon another housekeeper was employed. We had five housekeepers in total. Just as I got used to one, she would leave and another came. Sometimes I blamed myself when they left. I tried even harder to be 'good' – to do the right thing.

I became expert at adapting to their differing requirements and reading their moods. Always reserved, I'd now become unbearably shy. Communication was reduced to responding to questions, but they needed to be the 'yes' or 'no' kind and not relate to emotions. One asked me when I missed my mum most – at night? Such questions were unanswerable.

How could I describe the constant aching emptiness …the utter loneliness?

No – I couldn't look in – I had to keep busy.

So I filled my waking hours with activity. I collected English coins and foreign stamps. I made puppets and wrote scripts to perform with them. I learnt how to do conjuring tricks. I went swimming and taught myself to dive. I perfected handstands, headstands, skipping…

We lived in Wickham Avenue which backs on to Nonsuch Park. I loved the park and I walked and cycled around it. I explored plant and animal life and set up a Nature-lovers club for my friend, Jackie, and her sister. In summer I sometimes camped in the garden to watch the birds in the early morning.

I took out books from the library about dogs and obedience training, table tennis, photography and flower arranging! I got loads of 'Observer's Books' and 'I Spy' books and went to London Museums for more information. I played the recorder and the piano and sometimes composed 'music'. At Girls' Brigade I received loads of badges, identifying my 'achievements' in many of these areas. I also worked on the Duke of Edinburgh Award. With Richard I would spend hours in the holidays playing board games and many different card games.

I lived life to the full, throwing myself into each new activity. It was another form of escape from the emotions I couldn't handle. Once buried, they could be forgotten – or nearly.

My father, brother and I visited the grave fortnightly. I didn't enjoy going. It didn't help me. My grief was too well locked away. Or perhaps it was an uncomfortable reminder of all I was trying to run from. Once my friend Jackie was staying with us and asked why we were going. I couldn't answer her, but it was unthinkable to ask. I didn't query such things – I just conformed and passively accepted whatever my father decided. I think he felt it was our duty. I read the biblical inscription,

> *'O death, where is thy sting?*
> *O grave, where is thy victory?'*

I knew the real bit of my mum wasn't in the grave. *She* had gone straight to heaven and hadn't been stung by death but *what about me?*

I thought about life and death. What did it mean to be stung by death? Why was my life miserable? Other children were mostly happy – I was different. I couldn't verbalise it but my sense of insecurity and insignificance had been fuelled by the lack of communication. If I really mattered people would tell me what was going on.

My unhelpful strategy of silence meant no one else knew what I thought or felt. So no one knew the lies I believed and no one could correct my misunderstandings. Guilt clung to me. Did I blame myself for my mum's death? Or was it guilt over my weird responses of not crying and not talking? I was in a vicious circle in which suppression fed guilt which led to further suppression. My low self image was reinforced as I constantly repeated, 'I lose everything. I make a mess of everything. I'm no good at anything.'

My teen years were hard. Friends complained of their mums. I would have loved one to complain of! They were good friends and they could have helped me but I felt odd and isolated from them. Bizarrely, a sense of shame clung to me as if my mum's death was my fault.

My loss aggravated the usual teenage issues of identity and low self-esteem. It was hard to face anyone! I felt so buffeted that the slightest reproach, an unfeeling stare, a look of exasperation –threw me into yet another abyss of rejection, of insignificance and of agonising self- consciousness.

I ached for a normal family life. I found it only in books. They were my refuge. In my fantasy I could recreate the security for which I yearned.

I delighted in the countryside – the trees and grassy fields invited me to a peace for which I was restlessly searching. And so it seemed that the very author of creation was wooing me. Could I trust him to be always there for me? The loss of my mother was a mystery, yet I sensed God's love for me. My tentative faith then, like all my thoughts and feelings, was very private. So it was a major decision to be baptised publicly at seventeen.

It was a life-changing event. Prayer became conversation with a friend and I started falteringly to share my inner world. But many emotions were too well hidden even from myself. A shroud of dreamy hopelessness seemed to wrap itself around me, insulating me from the full range of emotions. My inner world was grey and unfeeling. Could I move on from the past? How could I connect again with my feelings?

I suspect I internalised anger and turned it against myself, making me feel even more unworthy of God's love. It was easily substantiated by my childish reasoning, 'If I were good enough, surely people wouldn't abandon me!' It seemed obvious that I was at fault. After all adults were always right, weren't they? And yet I had a sense that, despite all the 'evidence' to the contrary, God did love me and did want the best for me.

My mum's death led to another problem. Ten years afterwards my dad was still deeply impacted by grief and suffered from severe depression. Richard was living away and taking his university finals. I was alone with my father. Roles were reversed and I, feeling hopelessly inadequate, attempted to care for him.

Nothing I said made any difference. His negativity swamped me. Life was horrendous and unbearable. I started fantasising about putting my head in the gas oven. Suicide was very attractive. Two thoughts prevented me. One was the sneaking suspicion that perhaps God had a plan for my life. The other was the realisation that killing myself would make things worse for my father.

But in the blackness, I cried out to God. And I found him, particularly in the Psalms. The writers voiced the emotions that I didn't allow myself to acknowledge but that resonated deep within.

My brother, Richard, returning from university, was horrified at Dad's deterioration. Dad was admitted to a psychiatric hospital for a few weeks. It was confirmed that loss was a significant factor in his illness.

That September Richard arranged to stay at home with him while I went to a teacher-training college at Salisbury called the College of Sarum St. Michael. This was situated in the Cathedral Close. The Cathedral Close was a quiet area surrounding the Cathedral with a series of beautiful old buildings originally built to accommodate clergy and craftsmen serving in the Cathedral.

I had chosen Salisbury as being roughly half way between my home in the London borough of Sutton and Cheam and Aunty Ruby's home in Somerset. The College of Sarum St. Michael was an all girls' college with its roots firmly in the past – a bit like an old-fashioned boarding school with strict rules. But it had a reputation for excellence and it felt safe. Meals were cooked for us and provisions for Saturdays handed out. I can still smell the freshly baked buns given us every day with our midmorning tea!

It was exciting to be with other girls my age – to be free from feeling I was different from everyone else. Conversation revolved less around mums and family life. It was a chance to leave behind my grief-stricken childhood and my adolescence overshadowed by my father's mental illness. It was a new start.

I was placed in lodgings in a terraced house in the city with another student called Alison. I was delighted to discover that she too was a Christian. We immediately established an amazing rapport – a friendship I still treasure.

The following two years we shared a room at the top of Audley House in the Cathedral Close. We were privileged to have a stunning view of Salisbury Cathedral and the magnificent cedar trees in its grounds. The Close was a delightful tranquil haven in the hustle and bustle of this lively historic city. Its peace was strangely symbolic of our college motto 'In quietness and in confidence shall be your strength'. And the reassuring chimes of the Cathedral clock (apparently the oldest working medieval clock in the world) were a sound I never forgot.

But my friendship with Alison was the most precious gift of all. We talked for hours and hours. We prayed together and encountered the Holy Spirit together, inviting Him to fill us.

I began to trust Alison. She helped me open up some of my hidden thoughts and feelings – parts I had barricaded from the outside world. But the grief itself was still closely guarded. Or was it out of reach?

Yet Salisbury has a significant place in beginning my healing process. Both my relationship with Alison and my experience of the Holy Spirit penetrated the essence of my being – an exploration of identity – a discovery of who I was. And just as the Cathedral Close is set apart – a sanctuary of healing peace yet with the mysterious awe of worship ... so, too, those college days were a set-apart time – a time of healing – a re-creation as I learnt to lower my defences and yield to God's purposes in my life.

After college I returned home. My father was doing better and Richard was still at home. A year later I moved a few miles to Cobham in Surrey to be part of a church called Cobham Christian Fellowship (later known as Pioneer People). This church was trying to follow a New Testament model of church by living 'in community'. This meant sharing our resources and our needs and trying to be open with each other.

It was in this context that a respected leader, Stuart, spoke to me about my mum. He sensed there was something wrong and that her death was impacting me in an unhelpful way. He felt I needed to forgive her for dying.

I was new to these things then. It was a surprise to me that God wanted to deal with something so far back in my life – fifteen years before. Of course, I knew she hadn't *chosen* to die. But as an eight-year-old I *had* felt abandoned. Had I felt *she*'d let me down?

Slightly mystified and yet sensing he was on the right track, I gladly let him pray with me. He verbalised my sense of abandonment – my desolation that she hadn't been there for me when I needed her and he took me through a prayer of forgiveness. I released sobs, wrenched from deep inside.

Was that it? This was new territory. Talking about my mum was easier. Shafts of light had entered my prison cell, giving me glimpses of the shadows from which I'd hidden for so long.

I enjoyed the new teaching I was receiving but it challenged me. It threatened my carefully shielded inner world. It was time to face up to the truth.

There was teaching on acceptance – God's unconditional acceptance of us and therefore our need to accept one another just as we are. Was there something the matter with me? Perhaps it didn't matter – God totally accepted me. Gerald Coates, one of the leaders of the church, would often quote, 'God loves us the way we are but He loves us too much to leave us that way.'

I began to trust that God really did accept me – a delightful contrast to the accusing voice that was so familiar. I was used to attacking myself about everything. I was still tempted to look for identity in ways I helped others, like babysitting. But I was beginning to believe that other people appreciated me for who I was– not just for what I did.

Often the teaching would stir up questions. I belonged to a small group meeting in a home. This was an ideal place to air the questions. I had so many. It was a source of amusement! But it was good for me to probe and investigate – a refreshing change from the pervasive passivity that had sucked the life out of my childhood.

What about my inner prison? What about my habit of locking up my feelings deep inside? That strategy might have appeared to offer protection in the past. But God was challenging me now to be 'crystal clear' as a current song expressed it. I didn't find it easy – especially when I was upset. Withdrawal had become such an automatic response. But with painful embarrassment I tentatively began to say how I felt. Could I really trust other people again?

Sometimes I *was* let down. My habitual response was to blame myself. It was many years before I realised that blaming myself had become a snare. It meant I could avoid facing the issues where I needed to forgive others.

And when I *was* at fault?... Then I would wallow destructively in my failure, taking a perverse delight in my sense of worthlessness. I called myself names and told myself off to punish myself. My self-loathing took me to such depths of despair and despondency that I felt cut off from God. It was yet another snare.

Again it was the Psalms that rescued me. I identified with David's torment and then allowed God to take me, like David, on a journey back towards trust in God. I learnt to receive God's forgiveness and then to forgive myself.

I started to write my *own* 'poetry' or reflections. (A small selection is included in Appendix B.) As I invited God's perspective, my writing often followed the pattern of the Psalms in taking me to a place of peace and faith. I started to see where my thinking was out of line with God's. Deeply entrenched mindsets were challenged and slowly eroded. Could it be that my prison had a gate after all?

Sometimes my mind felt like a flow of painful streamers – each colour piercing as it passed through my consciousness. My every awareness was heightened. Could my agonising sensitivity actually have a positive aspect and be creative?

It was through the church that I met Malcolm. From the start the relationship brought a deep sense of peace and we were soon married. What would this mean for me? Church leaders encouraged me that marriage would heal some of the pain from my past. But they warned that hidden areas of need might also surface. So marriage wouldn't solve all my problems – it might raise more!

Aunty Ruby gave us a contribution to the deposit on a house. It needed rewiring and treatment for damp and it had no heating

– but it was home and we were grateful. Malcolm worked hard to make it liveable and redecorated it.

In the midst of the chaos I became pregnant! We were thrilled but my emotions weren't always predictable. There were some evenings when I felt so bereft.

Why did I feel so miserable? Was this hormonal or something more sinister? How would I cope with being a mum? Would my own lack of mothering create problems for my child? I knew my healing was not complete. I was looking for Malcolm to meet needs that could only be met by God.

But I couldn't be negative for long. Malcolm always spoke positive words. He encouraged me that life was good and that I would manage fine. So different from my father! My father always worried about everything and spoke so negatively.

Malcolm contradicted the negative comments that had been so much a part of my upbringing. In fact he often refused to listen to them. Once he said, 'I don't think I'll ask you any more about your day – I only get a tale of woe!'

I didn't find that easy. Was Malcolm being unsympathetic? Was he impatient? Did the things that bothered me not concern him? Didn't he understand? I had a choice. There were days when I preferred to wallow in my misery.

But on my better days I knew his response could help me. If I chose to give a positive report on my day, it would help deal with the deep-seated negativity that clung to so much of what I thought and spoke. Yes – life was good. Grief and sadness need not pervade it. That was just something in my past. I could move on.

I was taking big steps towards freedom. Or so I thought. I didn't know the journey would be so complex. Or that grief would touch our family again.

What helped me?

🐾 Receiving a present after my mum's death that she had chosen

What didn't help?

◊ Not being told about my mum's illness and that she might die

◊ Being taken to school the morning I was told of her death with no time to take in the news or to grieve

◊ Being taken to see Father Christmas instead of going to the funeral

◊ Believing there was something wrong with me because I didn't have two parents

◊ Keeping my feelings to myself and not talking about my mum

◊ My father's inability to handle his own grief and let me express mine

What could help?

👣 An understanding response from teachers – accepting lower performance– especially following absence from school

👣 Hospital visits

👣 Being told about what is going on – especially knowing more of the seriousness of the illness and that death is possible

👣 After the death – why death occurred and the events surrounding the death

👣 Inviting questions about the death – why it had happened – pursuing conversation

👣 Staying at home when told of the death so there is time to take in the news and be involved in the funeral arrangements and conversation of family members

👣 Being encouraged to cry

👣 Opportunity to attend the funeral

👣 Exploration and expression of feelings

🦶 If prayer is valued and appreciated, praying as a family to foster intimacy and the opportunity to see faith outworked in daily life

In subsequent years

What helped?

🦶 As my relationship with God developed, learning to be more honest with him and with myself and with other people

🦶 Reading the Psalms – finding in them a way to communicate the emotions I needed to express

🦶 Friends with whom I could begin to express my innermost feelings – especially my friend Alison

🦶 Becoming involved with a church where people accepted me but cared enough to challenge me to go deeper in a right response to my mum's death

🦶 Forgiving my mum for dying

🦶 Writing poetry/reflections to express what I was feeling and to find God's perspective

🦶 Having positive people around me (e.g. Malcolm)

2 *Michael*

Well our baby was born – a boy. We named him Jonathan. Two years later we had a girl, Rachel.

I wanted my children to be better prepared for death than I had been. I explained to Jonathan when he was very young that, after we die, we come alive again. He looked at me seriously and asked, "Have you come alive again yet Mummy?"

So I tried to explain about going to be with God and people who were still alive wouldn't see us. We would never cry or get hurt. We would be really happy and have a lovely time.

At five Jonathan loved his bunk beds. Every visitor to the home was 'treated' to a viewing. As I tucked him into bed one evening, he asked, "Will there be bunk beds in heaven?"

"Oh yes – really nice ones," I responded. We'll have all the good things we've got now and even better things as well."

Afterwards I analysed my answer. Was I encouraging a materialistic heaven? But I was sure that at the heart of his question was, 'Will heaven be as good as what I've got right now?'

I found a book entitled, 'What happens when we die?' which echoed my thoughts. We bought the book for Jonathan for Christmas, when he was nearly six. It joined his collection of favourites.

We had originally wanted three or four children. Glimpsing the enormous amount of work that goes into rearing each child, we were settling for two! Suddenly to our surprise I found I was pregnant.

The sickness began even earlier this time. Remembering how sick I'd been with Rachel, I was thinking, 'Oh no – eight more months of this!' Suddenly a voice broke in on my thoughts and said, 'It doesn't have to be like this.' Was this God speaking? Until that moment I didn't know it was possible to be healed of pregnancy sickness.

I felt very sick but I forced myself to focus on Jesus on the cross – the basis for the healing. Amazingly the nausea left me – I continued to remain free from it throughout the pregnancy. Having been sick at least four times a day with Rachel, this was really a miracle. It seemed God's hand was on this pregnancy from the beginning.

The baby was due around Christmas. Rachel was starting school the following January – probably around the time she would start to get bored with having a baby around. We welcomed this new life, praying fervently that both children would accept this baby too.

At that time babies were induced if they were due at Christmas. So on December 17th I was taken into hospital. Stuart (the church leader who had suggested I forgive my mum for dying) and his wife, Jayne, had become very close friends. Jayne had given me a verse – 'In all your ways acknowledge him and he will make straight your paths.' Informed that the baby was at an awkward angle, I took the verse literally and prayed for a straight path of delivery! This helped and I managed to give birth without drugs – a new experience for me.

It was a boy! We were glad, knowing Jonathan would respond better to a boy and Rachel would mother the baby – boy *or* girl. As I looked at this seven-pound baby, I felt there was something indefinable of the anointing of God on him. 'There's a man of God!' I declared – I hadn't felt like this about the others. Malcolm agreed – there was something special about him. Was this why I'd known God's supernatural intervention both in the pregnancy and the delivery?

The sound of carols filled the delivery room. This reminder of the Nativity seemed a fitting welcome for my baby. I was glad

I wasn't in a stable. I'd lost a lot of blood and found myself wondering if the hay had been useful for mopping up!

Birth congratulation cards arrived with Christmas cards and I continued to identify with Mary. We went to Malcolm's parents in Walsall over Christmas. Malcolm's father was struck by my love for Michael. He remarked to Malcolm's mum, 'I know she loved the others but she's like the Madonna with this one.'

It was true. I did love Michael intensely. It dawned on me that I couldn't hold on to him so tightly forever. One day he would leave home. I needed to be prepared for that separation. I consciously gave him to God but I thought we had another eighteen years together.

Jonathan and Rachel took to Michael instantly. There was a special bond between Jonathan and Michael – despite nearly seven years between their ages. Jonathan looked forward to the day he would play football with Michael. Rachel loved to hold him but, at four, often needed reminding to support his head. She liked the way he held her little finger.

One day he had a cold. Being snuffly he had a little trouble feeding. The Health Visitor came. She weighed him and assured me that he was putting on weight so there was no cause for concern.

The next day Jonathan had mumps. I rang the doctor to see if there were any precautions I needed to take with Michael. I was again reassured – he was too young to catch it.

That evening Malcolm picked up the book 'What happens when we die?' to read to Jonathan and Rachel. Malcolm had been off work with 'flu and I joked, 'Aren't you feeling so good tonight?' Malcolm read a little of the book and put it aside to continue another night.

The next day Michael was crying a little more than usual. It was snowy. Rather than take him out I left him with Malcolm and Jonathan while I collected Rachel from school at lunch-time. After lunch he enjoyed being held and he looked round the room while I fed him. Rachel had a ballet lesson so I took Michael with me, wrapping him up well and hoping the motion of the pram would settle him. He was soon quiet.

After ballet I quickly got the tea and picked him up for his feed. 'What a good boy you've been!' Then I looked at his face. I stopped short in horror. Something was very wrong.

'Malcolm, come quickly,' I gasped. He was sitting at the dinner table with the children at the other end of the room. My legs had frozen – I couldn't move. It was a scene that would be forever etched on my memory and I would replay many times. In that bewildering moment my whole world had stopped. I would never be the same.

'Shall we get a doctor?' I asked. But even as I spoke there was a sickening realisation that it was too late. This deathly pale face with dark blotches was so unlike my Michael, I knew only God could step in now.

The children joined us. There was no question of distancing them – we were in this together. The four of us stood there calling out to God – a desperate cry for help. Michael remained motionless, but a blanket of peace momentarily encircled us. It cocooned me from the panic, which, if I looked aside, threatened to take me over. Jonathan remembers it as a special time of closeness – so good to be together.

Into my mind flashed the recollection that our neighbour was a doctor. I pulled on my boots and rushed round. He tried to resuscitate Michael. I was thankful for his perseverance – it was painfully obvious there was no response. But it was a precious few minutes to grasp the facts. My baby who I'd fed just two hours before had inexplicably died.

In disbelief I looked at that tiny body. How could it have happened? What had gone wrong?

Jonathan looked devastated. I put my arms around him and said, 'It's OK to cry'. He did.

But I felt helpless to express *my* emotions. I was trying to carry something too big to get my hands around. It was so heavy that it sapped all my strength, tearing me apart inside. I felt so weak. How would I ever carry this weight of grief?

That very evening my church was holding a meeting for emotional healing. I had planned to go. Now it was out of the question. It was a time to be together, to comfort one another and to try to take in what had happened.

But from deep within me came a cry to God, 'Emotional healing – that's what I need!' Was healing really possible? Would I one day recover?

I was still looking at that little body. How could it be that this baby I'd loved so much was gone? How strange that just a few days before I'd anticipated his leaving home! Now as I looked at him – separated from me years earlier than I expected, some words from the Bible dropped into my mind,

'The Lord gave and the Lord has taken away. Blessed be the name of the Lord.'

Strange words! Harsh and cruel I'd once thought them – as if we were at the mercy of a capricious God who gave with one hand and took away with the other. Part of me still wanted to reject them on those grounds. Where was God in all this? Had he taken my baby? I'd *thought* God was on my side. Or was it some disastrous mistake, which had slipped through his fingers? My emotions were trying to translate pain into questions – questions I'd never tried to answer so personally before.

But now I saw Job's words in a new light. He'd seen something. He'd suffered a far, far greater loss – all his children at a single blow. But he'd recognised that God didn't owe him anything.

Job's words were an expression of worship. He was saying to God, 'Whatever you give or don't give – whether I know your blessing in my life or not – it doesn't alter who you are. I'm yours and all I've got is yours. You are worth it all.'

In echoing these words I resonated with that same sense of worship. I didn't understand what had happened but God was still God – still worthy of worship. God only did good things. Of course he hadn't taken my baby. Death wasn't a part of his plan of creation. It was as ugly to him as it was to me. But when evil entered the world it brought with it decay, destruction and death.

So was Michael's death a random event simply because we live in a fallen world?

I reflected on the mystery of his short life. He'd been a bonus – a special gift we'd treasured. He'd given us five weeks of joy. Gratitude welled up to God for giving me the privilege of borrowing him. In the bombarding grief that followed I wasn't always so objective but in those first few minutes I saw clearly that I was owed nothing.

I couldn't take my eyes off that little body. It had been so precious but now looked so weirdly different. In a flash of understanding I saw this wasn't Michael! It was just his body. Like a shell. He didn't need it any more.

'Michael isn't there,' I said to the children. We all agreed it didn't even look like Michael.

Then I saw so clearly where Michael really was. It was a picture in my mind but so vivid and so vibrant. For that moment, it was more real than the physical body lying limp before me.

What I saw was Michael lying in the arms of Jesus, alert and *smiling*! Never again would he cry! He was having all the milk and cuddles he wanted. Jesus himself was looking after him with warmth and tenderness.

It was easy to tell the children this. In the midst of my grief I felt a confusing excitement – a strange sense of wonder. Yes our loss was immense. But for Michael it was only gain. He had had all the love we could give him in five weeks and now he was in the arms of one whose love far surpassed mine. Those loving arms would never ever fail him.

There was a hurricane of emotion to come. But for the moment a supernatural peace embraced me, freeing me to focus on my children. My heart ached for them. What would this do to them? Would they ever recover?

I was particularly concerned for Jonathan. He'd been so thrilled to have a brother and was so caring towards him. That special bond, without warning, had been painfully ripped apart.

The doctor's wife, our neighbour, came and helped us finish giving the children their tea. Some yogurt had got spilt. It was a welcome distraction.

The children's bed time was approaching. A story was part of the nightly ritual. Jonathan picked up the book begun the night before, 'What happens when we die?' – the book we had bought Jonathan the previous Christmas. How extraordinary that Malcolm had selected it the previous evening! Had God been preparing us as a family?

Malcolm attempted to read it but was soon engulfed by emotion. I continued, for the moment detached and calm. We tucked the children into bed, praying that God would erase any horror from their memories and wrap them in his peace. Amazingly they were soon asleep.

It was time to face *my* emotions. Everything was so ludicrously unreal. Was it all a nightmare? Couldn't I put the clock back and relive the last twenty four hours differently? Could this tragedy have been prevented? The present was too painful. So was the future. My only hope was to change the past to create a different outcome. But a sinking emptiness inside wouldn't allow me to escape in denial.

I was calm. Too calm, surely, I thought. The doctor had urged me to hold the body. It would help me cry.

It helped a little. I looked at the infected eye I'd bathed so often. That eye would never again weep. But it drew *my* tears. Memories of that caring routine wrung from me a compassion and a tenderness that now had no target.

This body was so cold, so stiff, so unreal. It wasn't my Michael – more like a waxwork model. I wanted to change his clothes. They'd belonged to Michael *alive* and Jonathan too had worn them. They went with life not death. How dare this cold stiff body wear them! How dare it masquerade as my Michael! A nightie seemed more in keeping– more impersonal. But I struggled to get the unyielding arms inside it.

We called Stuart's wife, Jayne, to share with us in our grief. 'Poor Jayne, she won't know what to say,' I said, suddenly acutely and oddly aware of the challenge this would be for her. Every sensitivity was heightened.

But then came the beautiful realization that nothing need be said. I thought of times when I'd anguished over what to say in the face of tragedy. Now a blazing insight informed me that words were of no consequence. How could they ever be adequate! All that was needed was to communicate love.

But *I* talked and talked. I rehearsed the events of the day. Yes he'd cried a little more. He'd taken a long time to feed. But he'd sat contentedly in my arms, looking around the room, gazing intently at the lights, the pictures. Was he storing up these memories? Does a five week old baby know he's going to die?

His death was still a mystery. A coroner had questioned us and warned me that I would feel guilt. I certainly did. I went over and over my actions that day. It was only two days since the Health Visitor's reassurances over his cold. Had I bumped him, suffocated him, or missed a vital symptom?

Stuart and Jayne prayed with us. I didn't want to suppress grief like I had with my mum. So Stuart prayed that I would cry and release the grief.

I expressed the guilt I felt. Stuart declared God's verdict was 'Not guilty.' For that moment I believed it. No, I didn't have to add a burden of guilt to my grief like I'd done with my mum. I hadn't neglected Michael. I'd given him my best care.

Bizarrely too, Stuart, not knowing of my response, echoed the same words from Job,

'The Lord gave and the Lord has taken away. Blessed be the name of the Lord.'

How extraordinary! They weren't the most comforting of words but hearing them repeated was mysteriously reassuring. However baffling, it reminded me that Michael's death had come through the filter of God's loving hands. As with Job, the suffering was from an enemy source but God had set the limits.

Did God think I could cope with this? How astonishing! I felt so weak.

We went to bed. For the first time in five weeks my sleep wouldn't be broken by night feeds. But tonight how grateful I would have been to hear Michael's cry! These were dangerous thoughts. I stepped back quickly as from a lift with a shaky floor that wouldn't take my weight. I'd end up falling into a self-pity from which I might never recover. I must be positive. I was tired. Why not be grateful for the chance to sleep?

But sleep was not so easy. In fact for Malcolm and I broken nights were to feature in our lives for weeks. Sometimes we left the heating on, knowing it would be 'one of those nights'. We often passed like shadows, Bible in hand, seeking comfort from God.

But that night, each time I shut my eyes I was bombarded by the horror of the death scene. Guilt compounded it with nightmarish force. Everything I'd done and hadn't done stood out like pictures in a children's pop-up book, confronting me accusingly. There were a million things I could have done wrong. How could I ever have doubted my guilt?

Logic had left me. There would probably be only *one* cause for guilt. But I'd bumped him *and* suffocated him *and* neglected him in a thousand other ways.

Focusing on these pictures, I'd lost God's verdict. But I found in Malcolm a refuge from myself. He patiently reassured me again and again.

But other questions hurled themselves at me like waves that threatened to throw me headlong. No sooner had I jumped one, another would be waiting for me. It seemed only a matter of time before I drowned in them.

Where was God when this happened? Wasn't he my friend? How did he expect me to feel? How could he allow it? Why had he given me a gift only to take it away again? Was it my incompetence that had wrecked his gift? Was it anything to do with big prayers I'd prayed about giving God everything I had?

Choices lay starkly before me. I could accept God or reject him. What had happened I could never change. But I *could* choose my response. I could choose to be grateful for what I still had. Or I could become bitter and self-pitying.

Again and again my lifeline was that God hadn't changed. I recalled the times I'd experienced his compassion and his gentleness – times he'd spoken to me, times words of Scripture had jumped off the page. Even the distorting pain of Michael's death couldn't tip the scales against all I'd experienced of God's love for me. I held on too to the bigger picture of all I knew of God's character from the Bible – a heritage of thousands of years where people had found God loving and faithful.

Slowly I realized that the questions were irrelevant. I might never understand. It was a time to trust.

What could I gain from blaming God? If I rejected him, how could I receive his love? I needed God more than ever to help me through my grief. To lose my trust in him would be a greater loss than Michael's life. What would be left? I would lose everything that gave my life meaning and quality.

And as I chose to trust him, these words dropped into my mind, 'I will never leave you or forsake you.' Whatever God had allowed the enemy to take from me, I could never be robbed of *God's* love and presence. He was looking after me and he always would. It was a promise of hope that I clung to that night and one that was to sustain me for days and weeks ahead.

We got little sleep. But it was so good to be together. It was a special time of closeness – a time to receive each other's love. We shared our grief. We cried. We clung to each other. We talked. We prayed. We were so grateful to know God, to have each other and to have two lovely children.

Rachel's first words next day were, 'Where's Michael?' Oh no! Had she dismissed it all as a nightmare? I explained that he'd died but that Jesus was looking after him. 'Oh I know that,' she responded. 'But where's his body?'

I explained that the coroner had taken it to find out why he'd died. She was satisfied. It was peculiarly comforting to realise that even at four she'd adopted our vocabulary and could distinguish between Michael and his body.

I was acutely aware of the physical effects of grief. There was that familiar lump of pain in the stomach – the soreness in the throat, the shallow breathing. Every nerve was extra sensitive. Simply walking around the house hurt my shoulders and my arms as well as my legs. Everything I touched brought pain to my fingers – a sharp reminder that my body – my whole self was weakened, suffering, helpless.

It was a day of visitors. The word had got round quickly. Close friends called round. Others rang. Still others dropped notes through the door.

The love of our friends touched us deeply. When we'd got married our friends had shared with us in our joy. Now they were identifying with us in our grief. People were praying for us. It felt as solid as a wall.

The personal visits meant a lot. If I saw someone dropping a note through the door, I rushed out to thank them and invite them in. I hope I didn't upset them – I'd learnt from my childhood grief for my mum how easily a barrier of embarrassment could grow. I didn't want Michael's death to be a taboo subject. I wanted there to be openness even if it was painful. I knew too that talking would bring me healing.

But I didn't want people to feel that *they* had to say anything. Their words weren't important. In fact it was sad when people felt they had to come up with wise sayings or avoided us because they didn't know what to say. I simply needed to receive their love.

Out of habit I had a coffee each time I made one for a visitor. I'd lost touch with any signals from my body regarding food or drink – I was trying to remember what was normal. But then I realised that extra fluids weren't helping. I had breastfed Michael and the milk had built up and I was throbbing. My whole body was in mourning – the physical was an outward expression of the emotion inside. I was full to bursting with love and maternal care that I desperately wanted to pour into my baby. But there was no baby to receive it and the pain was acute.

But, despite the tenderness, I wanted to receive the love that people offered me. As our friends embraced us, it was as if God's arms were comforting me. Every embrace imparted love and healing however excruciating physically.

Malcolm went to get some medication to dry up my milk. But in a daze – the stupor of grief – he walked through the glass shop window of the chemist's. He broke his nose. It was a painful reminder that we needed our friends to look after us.

The tears were flowing freely now. Every memory and every thought triggered off another flow. Every loving letter and card – every bunch of flowers started me off again. I was grateful. I could feel their healing power.

I didn't want to subject my children to the full outpouring of my grief. But nor could I hide it completely from them – I think rightly so – they needed a model of grief. 'Why are you crying, Mummy?' they asked. 'Is it because of Michael?' Inwardly I marvelled that there could be any question in their minds.

But I simply responded, 'Yes, I know he's really happy with God. I just feel sad because I'm missing him.' This was hard to say but oddly helped. It was only *our* loss. Michael was really happy. It was good to keep declaring this out loud. My grief was natural. But taken out of the context of Michael's happiness, it could lead me into self-pity – a selfish bewailing of my loss oblivious of the fact that Michael was experiencing life in all its fullness.

I thought of Jesus' words,

'Take my yoke upon you and learn of me, for my yoke is easy and my burden is light.'

The yoke was responding in God's way – in this case declaring the truth of Michael's happiness. Sometimes that seemed hard and unnatural. But as I took it rather than following my natural inclinations, it seemed to fit surprisingly well. I'd thought I was doing God a favour! In fact *I* was the one who benefited.

As for the guilt, it *was* a relief when the coroner rang. The post mortem revealed pneumonia. Apparently it strikes a tiny baby so quickly not even a doctor could have done anything. Maybe I wasn't to blame after all. I knew I had a choice to make. I could believe God's verdict, which tallied with the coroner's, or I could stubbornly hold on to my guilt.

Thankfully I chose to let it go. I still occasionally battle with an accusing thought, 'Surely I should have noticed something wrong when I fed him just two hours before?' But I have to hang on to my memory of Michael feeding well, albeit slowly, alert and happily looking around the room. I have to reassure myself that I'd checked out the mumps and was looking out for cold symptoms. Admittedly Michael had cried more but a doctor doesn't want to see a baby every time he cries!

Strangely, five years later, we had another five-week-old baby who was ill. Lizzy, our youngest daughter had a heavy cold and her breathing was laboured. We took her to the doctor and, knowing our history, he ordered us to hospital for tests and observation. I wrote the following:

Five weeks and a day

Five weeks and a day
And Michael's life was snatched away.
Five years on...and another life
Is five weeks and a day
And does she battle to stay?

But no! This battle is mine.
Though fears still assail me,
I believe she is safe.
No! This fight is for my healing.
Will I let go my fears and my guilt?
Will I trust that with Michael I was not at fault?
That I would have given my all to save him?
Or will I continue to torture myself
For missing a vital clue...
Some symptom which had I recognised it in time
Would have saved him and freed me from guilt forever?

Yet You have freed me from guilt forever.
Give me grace to receive it
And trust You in Your purposes.

You are committed to my healing.
You will bring wholeness not just to Lizzy's body
But to my mind and emotions
As I face this
With You.

As it happened it *was* only a cold. We were discharged after a couple of days. I sensed God was reassuring me that I *was* able to notice when my children were ill.

Two days after Michael's death we had a very special time when we prayed together as a family. We were very conscious of our vulnerability. Death was a reality that could strike at any time – not just when we were old. A relationship with God didn't immunise us from suffering.

We stood in a circle – our arms around each other. I had a powerful sense of God in the middle of the circle. He was spreading his arm over us warding off all evil. Nothing would come near us unless he allowed it. Then I saw him outside of the circle with his arms around us all comforting us.

As I described this, Jonathan said, 'Yes. I felt two arms around me – yours and God's.' How exciting! Then Malcolm said that he'd seen a picture in his mind of a castle wall.

We were given a letter. It referred to the same day that we'd prayed together. Others had gathered and had been praying for us.

For Malcolm and Barbara:
Last Saturday, when Maurice was praying for you,
expressing his grief, at the early morning prayer meeting,
he asked God to wrap you all in his love. I saw your whole
family inside a circle of safety, which was full of God's love,
and comfort. Tenderness and grace were written there.
Encircling you was God's complete protection, strong like
a shield.

Much love,
Barbara M

It was a precious encouragement and a powerful confirmation.

As for Rachel, she had a dream about Michael. She'd seen Jesus holding him. 'He remembered to hold Michael's head up,' she told me excitedly. 'I always forgot. But he remembered.' I was moved by the way God was communicating directly with my children.

Some things were less helpful. I heard that a few people judged that I hadn't grieved properly. My responses didn't fit with their concept of grief. This was hurtful. What did they know of my tears and my pain?

It was perhaps for the sake of such people that it was suggested we didn't join the church in gathering that Sunday – 'some people wouldn't understand'. We were baffled – where we expected to find comfort we were excluded. Were we accommodating their grief or their misconceptions?

It was tempting to feel our needs should take priority – even that God should excuse us in terms of right responses – we'd done our bit! Perhaps there was a hint of self-pity – weren't we going through enough without making life harder? Whatever it was I found it took me in an unhelpful direction – away from God and into selfishness and bitterness. I didn't know who these people were but clearly I needed to forgive them.

We had a service of thanksgiving for Michael's life. The children were glad to be part of it. It was a lovely service and we were again touched by the support of our friends. Michael's death had impacted many people.

I discovered grief changed in its nature from day to day – sometimes from moment to moment. Sometimes I was back in the intensity of fresh grief but with no tears to alleviate it. Sometimes it was a dull empty ache.

Jonathan had got over the mumps. But there was no 'getting over' grief. Life would never be the same. I was changed forever. But I could choose whether I let it enrich me or embitter me.

Malcolm was back at work and the children back at school. But I was redundant – my job no longer existed. I was tossed in a moment from the constant day and night caring of a baby to an uncanny silence. I missed Michael deeply. I loved him so much and I longed to put my arms round him and tell him how very special he was to me.

But it was also a precious time. The picture of God with *his* arms round a smiling Michael made heaven more real and the unseen spiritual world more significant. I felt more aware of God's perspective.

I no longer took life and health for granted. I treasured my family and marvelled at the uniqueness of each person, longing for them to fulfil their full potential. I wanted more than ever to be a good mother to my children yet to guard against the over protectiveness that could so easily spring from fear. I had a sense of urgency that my life would count. I wanted to share God's love and help people to know him.

But I still had questions. What was Michael's life and death about? Why had we sensed something special about him? Had the world been robbed of a great man of God? Was the anointing on his life transferred to his death?

I may never know the answers to these questions. But what was apparent was that God wanted to reassure us of his love. It was a time not to demand answers but to learn to trust. Losing Michael was no reflection on God's love – he was the same God.

It was clear I was finding some ways of grieving more helpful than others. I could see how fear, horror, guilt, resentment or self-pity could aggravate the process. I was able to make much better choices than I had after my mum's death.

What helped?

🐾 Preparation for concept of death from reading book, 'What happens when we die?

🐾 My relationship with God over many years and especially knowing him in the pregnancy and birth and consciously giving Michael to God days before he died

- Being together as family – praying together, being vulnerable and finding strength in one another

- Looking to God for emotional healing – asking him to show how to grieve

- Scriptures – Job's words – concept of worship – realising God didn't owe me

- Talking

- Crying

- Holding/viewing the body to accept the reality of death

- Close friends praying with us

- Receiving love of friends – notes, flowers and especially embraces

- Choosing to turn from self-pity through gratitude and forgiveness

- Realising I couldn't change what had happened but I could choose my responses

- Choosing to trust when I didn't understand – holding on to what I knew of God and his love for me rather than demanding answers

- Malcolm's patient reassurances that I was not to blame

- Declaring that Michael was really happy – I was just sad because I was missing him

- Encouraging openness of communication

- Reassurance that I did take appropriate action when my children were ill

- Forgiving those who didn't understand my response to grief

- Journaling my questions and my insights and my responses to grief

♥ Writing the story of Michael to distinguish what I'd lost from what remained – what was him and what was me

What didn't help?

◊ Imagined guilt

◊ People avoiding me

◊ People trying to give answers

◊ People judging my grief response

◊ Not feeling free to meet with the rest of the church when gathered on Sunday before the funeral

◊ Self-pitying reactions to all unhelpful responses from people

3 *A Mum like I Wanted to Be*

We decided it would be healing to have another baby. I wanted the children to have pleasurable memories of having a younger brother or sister. I imagined them being asked about brothers and sisters and having to process, even if they didn't say it, 'We once had a little brother but he died...' I longed to lay a secure foundation for them to have their own children in adulthood.

As parents too, we wanted to complete our family on a happier note. Admittedly it would mean reliving memories of Michael, yet the end result would be healing. The joy of new life would eclipse some of the sorrow of grief.

Perhaps six months would be a sensible time to wait. I didn't want grief from Michael to affect a new baby in pregnancy. Time dragged disconcertingly in those early weeks after Michael's death. I had to keep reminding myself that my body had just given birth and needed time to recover.

I'd been following a post-natal exercise book. It had photos of the positions for the exercises – each complete with baby watching contentedly! Should I scrap the book? Yet I wanted to get my body ready to carry a new baby. I chose to look at the photos as a promise of the baby to come. But it wasn't always easy.

It was a strange time –a time of transition between the baby I'd lost and the baby I trusted I would have. It helped me to journal my questions and my thoughts. Michael had died in the midst of my 'maternal preoccupation' – the time after birth when the mother is totally absorbed in her baby. Breastfeeding had enhanced this oneness in the nurturing flow of my life into

Michael. I hardly knew which bit of 'me' had died. In writing about him, it helped me separate what was him and what was me – what was dead and what still lived – what was lost and what still held true.

It was a time of unpredictable emotions. At one point Malcolm said he didn't want another baby. Grief was affecting us differently in lots of ways and I recalled how after a loss of a child over one in two marriages breaks up. I knew it made sense to wait, but emotionally I wanted to have the baby *now* even though I knew Michael could never be replaced. As for having no more children ever! It would surely accentuate the loss.

I prayed. Every time it came to mind –sometimes it seemed a thousand times a day – I tried to hand it over to God. Next time we discussed it Malcolm was keen to have another baby. What a relief!

Thankfully too I soon got pregnant. We were thrilled and excitedly told the children. We went to Bournemouth for a seaside holiday. Everything was fine apart from some dizziness – probably my low blood pressure – always a problem for me in early pregnancy.

I was 14 weeks into the pregnancy when the hospital doctor expressed some concern. The baby wasn't as big as he expected and he queried whether I was pregnant at all. Certainly I hadn't much of a bulge but I remembered how the hospital had worried me about Rachel's size and she'd turned out fine, weighing 6 pounds 14 ounces. The hospital arranged for a scan to check out this pregnancy but I had to wait three weeks as scans were done at 17 weeks.

But ten days before this I started to lose blood. What was going on? I lay in bed wondering if this was a situation to stand against in faith. Surely I couldn't really be losing another baby! God wouldn't put me through that again, would he? Hadn't I passed that test?

I pored over words I'd been given a couple of weeks before (just before the hospital visit). They'd been spoken over me by Charles Slagle, a visiting prophet. Out of the three hundred people in the Village Hall he'd picked me out to stand. He'd never met me and knew nothing about me but felt he had a message from God for *me*.

'He's been making you feel like a mum like you've wanted to be...'

I certainly felt a mum. Pregnant with my fourth child that was hardly surprising! But what sort of mum did I want to be? He continued,

'It's been very, very hard because of the great grief that the Enemy has worked in your life with one who would be the youngest.'

I was convinced the words had come from God. The prophecy continued with the promise that God was healing the grief and appeared to be saying that he was giving me a child that he would raise. I'd been thrilled.

So I lay in bed clinging to these words with everything I had. But the bleeding continued. In fact it increased. Pains intensified like contractions. It was like giving birth but far far too early.

I was bewildered. Where was God in this? Why was he now so silent?

One night I lost a lot of blood – huge clots. And I was so weak with nausea and faintness that I needed Malcolm to help me to the bathroom. We lost all hope that I still had the baby.

Next morning I felt a bizarrely inappropriate sense of accomplishment. It was the same feeling I'd identified after giving birth. Was this hormonal? This time it mocked me. There *was* no baby and there *would* be no baby.

My scan appointment officially confirmed what we already knew. The hospital kept me in for a D & C. I read Psalm 139 – the verses David had written to express that, wherever he was, God was with him. I'd just been reading verses 9-10

'If I rise on the wings of the dawn,
if I settle on the far side of the sea,
[10]even there your hand will guide me,
your right hand will hold me fast.'

Then the needle for the general anaesthetic was inserted into *my* right hand. In my befuddled helplessness I sensed God reminding me that he was holding me fast.

It was the night of the violent storm of October 1987. I woke next morning to discover trees had crashed down everywhere. So stable, so established, so much a part of the landscape but tossed about as if by a capricious whim. The devastation outside matched the confusion in my mind. What was God doing? Nothing was certain any more.

Yet, an incomprehensible blanket of peace temporarily quietened me and I snuggled gratefully under his care. What had happened was no reflection of his love for me. I didn't understand it, but he would work out everything for good. So as I chose to trust him, the certainty of his love for me became like a great rock that no storm could ever shake.

Malcolm brought me home the next day. I felt weak in every sense and it took very little to trigger off tears. In frustration I looked at jobs to be done but all my strength had ebbed away. 'Why was I being so lazy?' I wondered guiltily. Was this hormonal too?

Suddenly it struck me I hadn't grieved. I'd accepted as a biological fact that one in five babies miscarries. But this was a *life* I'd lost. This was my precious baby! And one invested with such promise – one who was to take away my tears and bring me joy. So I gave myself permission to cry. I let the tears flow.

This time there were no phone calls. There were no notes through the door. People who knew me crossed the road when they saw me coming. Had I become an embarrassment? Like a leper should I ring a bell so people could avoid me? Why this conspiracy of silence? Only my closest friends spoke of it.

I felt shunned. Reason told me people just didn't know what to say. But my emotions cried out for hugs – for sympathy – for sharing in my grief. I was going through the same experience of loss and grief as I had with Michael. But where was the human comfort?

No *body* to bury, no one to talk to, no acknowledgement of the grieving process. What was I to do with my grief?

Fresh grief compounded the old. But worse! After losing Michael I'd felt God's closeness. This time I felt abandoned. Had I had any illusions after Michael's death that I had an inner strength to endure grief? God took care to shatter any such misapprehensions. I humbly acknowledged my vulnerability and inadequacy.

I was exhausted – mentally, physically and emotionally.

I wrote in a journal,

> *'I feel so tired – so desperately tired. I don't want to move. My body seems to cry out for more rest. The simplest task demands every effort of my will. There is no motivation to do anything that requires any movement of my body. Is this laziness? Or is it my body's simple response to grief? Is grief physically exhausting? Does grief masquerade as tiredness?*
>
> *Perhaps I just need time. Maybe rest for the body brings rest to the emotions. Perhaps I need to be and not try to do anything– not even try to understand everything.*
>
> *I need time to absorb what's happened – not just at the onset of grief but in its changing states. I know I have no resources in myself. I'd be deceiving myself to think I have the strength for this. I place all I am in God's hands and cling to him, trusting him to be everything I need. His strength is made perfect in my weakness.*

In quietness and trust is my strength

(Isaiah 30: 15)

[There was my old college motto again!]

> *My strength isn't in what I accomplish or in how strong I feel. It isn't in how I respond emotionally.*

My strength is in that deep-down trust in God –
that knowledge that he loves me, that he's on my
side and that he's working everything for my good.'

All I knew was that God was still God and he loved me. Sometimes I felt his love. Mostly it was just a cold fact I held on to.

I wanted to hide from the world – to retreat till the nightmare was over. But where could I go? My strong declarations of faith in God had subsided to whispers in my mind – barely more than intellectual assertions. My experience wanted to deny their reality. I faced the same question as I had with the loss of Michael – how could God do this to me? This time there were no words of comfort.

It was an effort to get up – an effort to do anything. To survive I shut down my reflective thinking and tackled jobs mechanically like a robot, hoping the familiarity would bring some comfort of its own. I worked through a housecleaning routine each morning – cleaning windows, bathroom and kitchen with the discipline of a military exercise. Everything was pointless so it was futile to look for reason in it and it seemed to keep Malcolm happy.

The past had a pain from which I was still hurting. A brighter future was still out of view. But the present was barren in more ways than one.

I was in danger of slipping into self-pity. In losing Michael, I felt God helped me respond to him in worship with the words, 'The Lord gave and the Lord has taken away. Blessed is the name of the Lord.' The picture of Michael smiling in the arms of Jesus had given me perspective – it was *my* loss but not Michael's. The awareness that others were grieving with me and sharing my burden expressed the truth that God too was partaking in my grief – reassuring me of his love.

But, after the miscarriage, the grief was harder to bear because it seemed unshared. The unspoken message I received was that people cope with miscarriages every day without making such a big deal of it. Others had their own lives to live and I shouldn't expect their help. And the tiredness? Perhaps I was just lazy.

Another challenge was the prophecy. What did it mean? I looked at the framework for those puzzling words. The prophecy began with a promise that God was guiding me and healing me and that I would hear from God how to free others. Then it explained that God would teach me to hear his voice for myself and to trust him. This was the context for the words,

> *'He's been making you feel like a mum like you've
> wanted to be. It's been very, very hard because
> of the great grief that the enemy has worked in
> your life with one who would be the youngest.
> The Lord is bringing a healing in your life now and
> he is giving you the ability to release and let him
> raise the child and let him do it through you and
> sometimes apart from you. And let him be your
> Dad too.'*

It continued with the promise that God was bringing adjustment to my whole body and my whole life. It encouraged me to ask God for more. I wasn't to settle for so little. I was to ask for a lot in order to have a lot to give away.

There was no implied certainty that I'd have a healthy baby subsequently. Perhaps the words that followed about God raising the child were in relation to Michael. God was reassuring me that he himself was raising Michael.

If these words also related to the miscarriage, then there was the same promise of healing from grief and God himself raising the child. Maybe God was reassuring me. I released the miscarried baby to him for him to 'raise', trusting him to heal my grief as he did so.

It's only in writing this chapter that I've felt that these words actually referred to my mum. Initially, as the words were spoken, I *had* received it that way. It addressed my concern that, not having been mothered myself, I would fail to be a good mother to my children and it reassured that, where my childhood had been cut short, God was bringing wholeness.

But then the leader of the meeting explained to everyone present that, earlier in the year, I'd lost a baby a few weeks old. Not unreasonably, he'd applied the word to this situation, not knowing of the loss of my mum. I'd given his interpretation more weight than my own. Certainly the grief from Michael, along with all I'd learnt about responding in grief, gave opportunity for God to begin a deeper healing from my mum – indeed the 'great grief' of my life.

God was giving a glimpse of how this grief fitted into his bigger plans for my life. He would heal my grief, and use me to bring releasing healing words to others. He wanted me to ask him for a lot so I'd have a lot to give away.

Even though my understanding of the prophecy was incomplete, I was beginning to trust God for himself even more than for his promises. His *words* I might misunderstand, but God himself would never let me down. There might be times when I wouldn't hear him speak or feel his presence, but it didn't change the fact that he was holding me in his love and grieving with me.

I knew how healing I'd found it to talk after Michael's death. Who could help me grieve now? I decided to search out others from my church who had had a miscarriage.

I came armed with questions. How did you feel? Were you conscious of grief? What helped heal the grief? Did talking help? In your experience was it a taboo subject socially? How did God help you?

I found people very willing to talk to me. They shared their sense of expectancy over their baby. They shared their silent shock, their bitter disappointment, their sense of being robbed. They shared their rationalising that it happens to a lot of people.

They shared their confusion. Had God tried to warn them? What about God's promises for this baby? Hadn't he spoken? They recognised that, though they had no answers, God was still trustworthy. As they cried, they knew God was grieving too.

Like me they'd found it hard to find people to talk to. No one wanted to know. They'd felt very alone. Each had felt she was the only person in the world to have a miscarriage.

One had been able to talk to several people and cried over every mention of babies. Every time she cried she'd invited God in again. She found this enabled her to release the grief and find God's healing.

Another was told that miscarriage is very common. 'It's no problem – just a little hiccup in life.' So it had seemed ridiculous to grieve. Three months later she was battling with depression. She kept taking time off work. It was her mum who said, 'I think this is to do with the miscarriage'. She spent the next two weeks grieving – constantly in tears.

Successive miscarriages had compounded the problem. People hadn't known what to say and had crossed the road to avoid her – just as I'd experienced. She found she had to make the first move, knowing that she needed their friendship. Inviting a friend to question her, drew out feelings and thoughts she'd never thought of sharing before. She also came to realise that God was grieving too. She knew her loss was not just 'matter' but a real human being – a child in heaven whom God was nurturing. She allowed her tears to flow whenever her emotions were stirred – seeing other babies or even their prams, seeing pregnant women, even someone saying something kind.

Yes, for me, it *had* helped me to talk to people. I no longer felt so alone. Our experiences of grief had much in common. Others had experienced the same pain of isolation. Guilt and accusation had pursued them too.

How frustrating that we'd all felt so alone! At a time when we'd needed to receive strength and support from one another we'd been separated. Embarrassment, independence, pride and social conventions had all played their part. The denial of grief had brought confusion to us and robbed the family of God of the strengthening which comes when 'we weep with those who weep'. In fact we'd felt rejected when we could have felt loved. We felt outcasts when we could have felt 'family'. We felt guilty and insecure when we could have felt affirmed and cared for.

As for myself, I found my tears would flow in church gatherings. As we sang songs of worship the presence of God turned on the tap. At first I was embarrassed. Why was I crying? But it felt therapeutic. It continued week after week and I learned to accept it as God's healing deep in my spirit – deeper than my mind and emotions could experience. Whether I was crying for Michael or for my miscarried baby or indeed my mum, I didn't know. The griefs had rolled into an aching emptiness that I longed for God to fill. Each time I cried I opened myself up to his healing love, knowing he understood.

So I ended 1987 having lost two babies in a year. It was a year I was glad to end. As we welcomed the New Year of 1988 a friend wished me a Happy New Year. What could I say that wouldn't dampen the moment of celebration for everyone? But I found the words trite and unfeeling. How could I be happy when two babies I'd loved so much were with me no longer! What would the New Year hold? Could I handle any more pain?

We waited the prescribed three months. Then I became pregnant again. My initial response was 'Yes but I've been here before.' Instinctively I wanted to protect myself from further disappointment. I was dragging my feet. One day it dawned on me that such negativity would rob me of the joy and anticipation which are so much a part of pregnancy. Could I respond differently?

After all, although fear and apprehension were such a natural response, how could I save myself anyway? I had no resources to cope. I said to God, 'If anything goes wrong this time, you'll just have to help me out.'

And so it felt like I was striking up a bargain with God. As a deliberate choice I would delight in this new life growing within me. But he would have to rescue me if anything went wrong. I found that, as I trusted him, I actually experienced a growing excitement. Wow! I could start to believe all would go well. Was I becoming a mum like I wanted to be?

Sometimes the pregnancies started to merge. It felt like a very long pregnancy. Elephants are pregnant for two years and as time went on, I too felt like a mother elephant and not only in size! In two and a half years there'd been only nine months when I hadn't been pregnant.

Finally our baby was born – a little girl. But not so little! Weighing over nine pounds, she was our heaviest baby and bigger than Michael had ever been. As a family we marvelled at her size and alertness and thanked God. We called her Catherine. We were grateful that her gender and size distinguished her from Michael from the start. It gave each a clearer identity so Catherine need not live in Michael's shadow.

The birth and early weeks brought memories of Michael flooding back. Sometimes asleep, she would lie motionless. Was she still breathing? In unguarded moments the memory would flash back of the evening I found Michael lying so very still.

The compulsion to monitor Catherine was so intense it felt obsessive. I had to stop myself checking on her every few minutes. In fact I was the one who needed checking! In holding myself back I consciously put her in God's hands, asking him to help me not be fearful and over-protective and to make me a mum like I wanted to be. And he did! I was soon amazed at my relaxed attitude and my confidence that Catherine would grow up strong and healthy.

Six years later a friend had a miscarriage. By then we also had our youngest daughter, Lizzy. As my friend shared her feelings, it triggered off memories I'd nearly forgotten.

A couple of days before she'd fully miscarried she'd had a picture of a baby at peace wrapped up in blankets in heaven. She felt this prepared her to let go of her baby. Another friend had a picture for her of a sun setting behind a tree in winter. Though stark and vulnerable, there was a sense of God's glory transforming the pain.

She wanted a simple 'service' to give focus to her grief. It was a special time when just six of us met in my home to share her grief and express our love. I read some Psalms including these verses from Psalm 31. The words reminded me of the physical weakness I'd known following my own miscarriage.

' *⁹Be merciful to me, O Lord, for I am in distress;*
my eyes grow weak with sorrow,

my soul and my body with grief.
[10]My life is consumed by anguish
and my years by groaning;
my strength fails because of my affliction,
and my bones grow weak.
[14]But I trust in you, O Lord;
I say, "You are my God." '

She read a poem she'd written that morning.

Little One

Little one, I longed to hold you and nurture you
You were part of me and the frailty of my flesh
I feel the grief that you are gone
But I know you are in the place I long for
That place of perfect love and peace
In the arms and care of your heavenly Father
In the beauty of His courts
Free from the suffering and corruption of this world
I know one who bore my grief 2000 years ago
On a cross
So I could be set free and to comfort me as I mourn
I know my present sadness will turn to perfect joy
When I see the one who bore my grief
And I see you again

Then we prayed for her and her husband and her two-year old son. He was playing with my daughter, Lizzy, who was the same age. It seemed very natural. Now she looks back at that time with appreciation and gratitude for her friends who stood with her and the sense of God's presence, giving her 'a taste of heaven'.

And for me… it was the service I hadn't had. It was another goodbye that took place 'better late than never'. It was the end of another chapter.

What helped?

- Reading Psalm 139 and believing God understood and accepted me and my responses even when I didn't understand myself

- Holding on to God's love for me, though I didn't understand what was happening

- Giving myself permission to grieve

- Letting the tears flow even when it seemed inappropriate (e.g. any mention of babies or during worship)

- Talking to others who had experienced a miscarriage

- Journaling my responses to grief

- House-cleaning routine

- My friend's service for her miscarriage

- Choosing to enjoy the next pregnancy rather than let the previous bad experiences rob me

- Choosing not to be obsessively over-protective

What didn't help?

◊ Misinterpreting the prophecy (this resulted in disappointment)

◊ Initially not realising I needed to grieve

◊ Consequent frustration with myself and false guilt and self-accusation

◊ Silence and isolation – people avoiding me

◊ Self-pitying reactions to all unhelpful responses from people

◊ Trying to understand and reflect on what had happened

◊ Lack of focus for grief – no body, no service, no public recognition of grief

What could help?

- Acknowledgement that this is a time to grieve
- Phone calls
- Flowers
- Cards and notes
- Hugs and sympathy
- Knowing others share the grief and are praying
- Service (like my friend had)

4 *Dad*

The first 16 months after Catherine's birth was a happy time. As well as my own pleasure in her, I really enjoyed Jonathan and Rachel's delight in this new baby. At eight and six they were old enough to appreciate her cuteness and marvel at each new development, yet young enough to enter fully into her toys and play. Perhaps, too, we all knew we could no longer take life for granted. She was all the more precious and we were so grateful that she was growing into a strong fun-loving toddler. We began to feel more secure as a family.

But by February 1990 my brother, Richard, and I could no longer deny that my father's health had begun to deteriorate. One day Richard, visiting him at his bungalow, reminded him of the story "The Chequer Board" by his favourite author – Nevil Shute. In that book, the central character is told that he has twelve months to live, and the book recounts how he spends those twelve months. Richard commented to Dad that we had no idea how much time he had left, but asked if he had any particular outstanding ambitions he wanted to fulfil. He didn't seem to have any.

It was a tricky time. Dad needed daily care and it was impossible for me to help while looking after my young family. Richard also had three children and his father-in-law was in hospital having heart surgery. Richard's wife, Miriam, was also awaiting an operation. It seemed the only solution was to pay for outside help for Dad. I arranged for carers who would check on him, give him a meal, make sure he took his tablets and do some basic cleaning.

In some ways I'd carried a sense of responsibility for Dad since his acute depression when I was in my teens. That period had left its mark. Dad had never fully recovered. And the father/daughter relationship had altered. We'd swapped roles. He'd become more dependent. I'd become more protective of him.

There was still much affection. I was grateful for all he'd done in my early years and for his ongoing care even while holding down a demanding job. But, from the time of his depression, I was aware of his vulnerability. Even at that early stage there was a sense of loss. He was no longer the father I'd once known.

Over the next few years there were other times when he'd been hospitalised for short periods. But it soon became apparent that, apart from drugs and the insulation from the pressures of life, there was little the hospital could offer. In fact the unpredictable behaviour of other inmates often outweighed its advantages. I became disillusioned. I felt I could achieve better results with a game of Scrabble. Sometimes I did.

At one stage he was no longer depressed. He never stopped talking and hardly slept. He had dozens of lists of things he planned to do but he couldn't really concentrate on anything. He started to spend money much more freely and became very argumentative. He was convinced he was well but we were more concerned than ever. What had happened to our patient, gentle easy-going father?

Finally his medical condition was diagnosed. We discovered that his condition was manic depressive and he'd entered the manic phase. In bipolar terms he'd gone to the other extreme. His medication was adjusted. Then he took a dip into depression. But eventually his behaviour and mood stabilised.

It was soon after this that I met Malcolm and we married. When Jonathan was born my father came to the hospital and bonded with him immediately. He marvelled at his perfection and was overjoyed to have a grandson. He'd recently retired and he took a lot of interest in Jonathan's first two or three years, savouring each new accomplishment.

We used to meet for Sunday tea. Dad had some fish in a pond in the garden. As we arrived he would say to Jonathan, 'Do you want to see a fishy?' He was thrilled the day that Jonathan, barely speaking, said on arrival, 'Want to see a fishy.'

On every visit to our home he would bring sweets for Jonathan … and for Rachel too when she was old enough. One day he visited when the children had just returned from a party. He was struck by their excitement over their party bags. Ever after he would give them each a paper bag of penny sweets or pick and mix and enjoyed their delight as they explored the contents. Those bags of sweets are one of Jonathan's special memories!

Dad very nearly remarried. At the age of 69 invitations went out for a wedding in May 1984. But he had second thoughts. Would it work? Had he lived too long alone? He suspected that his fiancée would be torn. Her aging mother wanted her daughter to herself and his wife-to-be found it difficult to refuse her mother's demands. Conflict was almost inevitable.

It was difficult. So often I'd talked him into going out or going on holiday when his instinctive response was to call things off when he panicked. Afterwards he'd been grateful. But this was such a huge decision – the consequences were so great. It seemed inappropriate for me to influence him. And he called off the wedding.

He threw himself into foreign travel. Over the next few years he ventured to New Zealand, Toronto, Mexico and South Africa. He had been in New Zealand at the time of Rachel's birth in 1982 and returned four years later at the time of Michael's death early 1987.

But now, early in 1990, he was no longer well enough to travel and seemed to have little quality of life. Each time I saw him I grieved over his deterioration. Travelling west on our journey home, with a heavy heart, I silently watched the sun setting behind the stark bare winter branches. I reflected that for Dad, too, his day was drawing to a close.

Life was becoming bleaker. I recognised a conflict within me. There was a reluctance to acknowledge this harsh reality. I could see it was futile and illogical but I longed for the return of days when he was stronger – when we weren't troubled by such morbid thoughts and with childlike oblivion could enjoy each day as if time and life were unlimited. I was desperately trying to cling to a past that was rapidly slipping through my fingers. The grieving process had begun but I resisted embracing it fully.

Perhaps that was natural. There's a detachment that's part of the grieving process – a letting go which can feel like a betrayal. After all he was still alive and I wanted to hold on to everything about him. To grieve fully seemed a rejection of the life and hope we still possessed. I wanted to remain positive. So how could I mourn? Grief conflicted with the desire to cherish the life that still remained.

Dad was diagnosed with Parkinson's disease. It was sad to see his movements so slow and restricted. It became apparent that the daily carer's visits were no longer adequate. He needed constant care. He went into a home – then another which suited him better. He soon needed even more nursing care and moved again.

I decided to spend a weekend streamlining his bungalow. Dad was always a hoarder and since his deterioration he'd thrown away very little. He even had neighbours' junk mail. And in the larder I found three empty Marmite jars! I wanted to 'declutter' to make it a little easier for cleaning. I was still clinging to a hope that Dad might return. In my more realistic moments I knew that this was a job that would need doing at some point. I preferred to do it before he died rather than after.

He went to Richard and Miriam's home at Christmas. He was cold and cuddled a hot water bottle the entire time. His birthday was soon afterwards – January 7th. He was 76. He came to *our* home then along with Richard and Miriam. I'd made a cake and we sang 'Happy Birthday'. But what did that mean? What quality of life was there to celebrate? He was barely aware of his six grandchildren who were sharing in the occasion. Did he have anything to live for?

He returned to the Home. He no longer enjoyed the social interaction. He was increasingly glad to retreat to his own room. So we bought him a portable television. But he found little to watch that interested him.

Less than a month later the Home rang to say he had pneumonia affecting both his lungs. We'd often rung the Home, enquiring after Dad, but this was the first time they'd rung us. Was that significant? In fact antibiotics cleared Dad's infection after all. But he was left very weak.

One evening we left all three children with friends while we visited him. A tape recorder was playing hymns in his bedroom. It felt peaceful. Dad was curled up in bed in the foetal position. I was struck by a bizarre parallel with pregnancy – a time of preparation for the next phase of his journey.

In his whole life he had never been more than 10 stone. Now he was just skin and bones. He opened his eyes. But he was no longer able to speak. There was something different about his features that I could only describe as a 'look of death.'

Was this my last chance to say goodbye? Or could I be mistaken? Embarrassment in case I was wrong held me back a little. Is it that the acknowledgement of death is not so easy with those we love? Or was this some vestige from my childhood – a lack of openness in handling death?

I held his hand and thanked him for all he'd done for me. I spoke of our happiest memories together – our holidays in the mountains of Spain. There was a responding light in his eyes. It reassured me he was hearing and understanding me. It seemed he was grateful too for these memories.

I recited Psalm 23 from the old King James' Version I'd learnt as a child. He seemed to draw comfort from the familiar words.

'The Lord is my shepherd;
I shall not want.
²He maketh me to lie down in green pastures: he leadeth me
beside the still waters.
³He restoreth my soul: he leadeth me in the paths of
righteousness for his name's sake.
⁴Yea, though I walk through the valley of the shadow of death,
I will fear no evil: for thou art with me; thy rod and thy
staff they comfort me.

⁵Thou preparest a table before me in the presence of mine
   enemies: thou anointest my head with oil; my cup runneth
   over.
⁶Surely goodness and mercy shall follow me all the days of my
   life: and I will dwell in the house of the Lord forever.'

I prayed with him. I told him when I planned to visit again. His eyes looked sad. I suspect he was trying to tell me there would be no more visits. But I wasn't ready to receive that. Or was I pretending for his sake? Who was protecting who? I no longer knew. I said goodbye and left.

The next morning the Home called me. Dad had died in his sleep early that morning. I'd half expected it yet I was still staggered by the finality of it. I quickly stepped into organisation mode. I left the children with friends again and met Richard at the Home.

Travelling over I identified a tinge of regret. I'd shied away from a complete goodbye. It had been my last chance and I'd missed it. Why had I expressed an expectation that we would meet again? I felt Richard had done a better job. He'd visited a lot over the last week. He'd recounted various incidents, thanked Dad for several things and apologised for others and had treated each visit as if it might be his last.

Dad looked peaceful. It helped. Clearly it was no longer an issue for him – if indeed it had ever been. It was simply my problem. Was I going to blame myself forever for the incompleteness of my goodbye? I chose to allow his peacefulness to dispel my feelings of guilt. I reassured myself that at least there had been some acknowledgement that life was coming to an end. It was a better goodbye than I'd known with my mum or with Michael or the miscarriage.

His look of peace comforted us in other ways. It was good to know that he would never be anxious or depressed again. Of course we would miss him but there was a sense that he'd lived his life and that in death he'd simply crossed the threshold into a richer, fuller and happier life. There was something more natural and fitting about this death.

I gave Richard a hug, remembering how healing I had found hugs after Michael's death. Perhaps too I wanted to share grief consciously with Richard after Dad's death. I wanted to avoid the communication difficulties I'd known after my mum's death. I didn't want any distancing between family members.

We shared the details of our last visits. I'd been his last visitor. Today was Valentine's Day – a day for couples to celebrate being together. We were glad to think of him being reunited with Mum nearly thirty years after they'd been parted.

The death certificate recorded the cause of death as old age with Parkinson's disease as a contributory cause. Perhaps 76 wasn't all that old but it was in marked contrast to the death of my mum at 45 and Michael at five weeks. Those deaths had been a shock, being unforeseen – unanticipated by me. I was much better prepared this time.

Or was I? I pondered on the same sense of unreality I'd assumed was from shock when death was unexpected. Why was it here again? Was it mocking me for my assumption that, because this death was predicted, it would be 'easier'?

I suppose death is always difficult however much anticipated. Was it something to do with its absolute finality that took my breath away? The dreams of full recovery – of even partial recovery were now forever laid to rest.

Yet there was a strange sense of liberation about his death. This was a new experience for me, though I dimly remembered from my teens my father talking about a 'happy release' when *his* father died. It was an odd mixture of feelings – relief that his suffering was over but tinged with guilt that *my* life would also be easier without the constant visits and concern for him.

Did I need to carry this guilt? I recollected that even on his birthday just five weeks before I'd observed there was little to celebrate. Life was no longer pleasurable or fulfilling for him. Why not be glad that his suffering was over? Why not be glad that he was now at peace?

Richard and I apportioned out the immediate tasks. As executor he took on the legal and financial responsibilities. So I took on the job of informing people and planning the details of the funeral service. We went to the undertakers together to organise the coffin and place and time of the funeral. It was therapeutic to make the plans.

I was conscious there were many people to inform. I collected Dad's address book and composed a letter. It was healing and strangely energising to summarise the events that had led to his death and also what he'd meant to us. I included these words,

> *'We are grateful for Dad's investment into our lives and for all his care and concern for us – especially in bringing us up without a mother. We were glad to see him living life to the full in his enjoyment of foreign travel even up to the last three or four years. It is only in the last eighteen months that his health has really deteriorated and he was struggling with living at home. We were so pleased to find in Eothen Nursing Home such a loving, caring atmosphere and we are very grateful for all they did for Dad in his time there – the final two months. They nursed him through pneumonia over the last few days, but it left him very weak and he died of 'old age'.'*

In response letters and cards streamed in. They put me in touch with a Dad I'd all but forgotten – a man appreciated for his wit and humour and his patience and compassion. People commented on his zest for life, his love of learning and his delight in words. He'd loved to carry around a big book and refer to it in fun as his 'light reading'. He was also remembered for his retelling of personal stories including his incredible recall of significant dates – not just the year but the month and actual day.

I'd had no letters when my mum died. Letters and cards after Michael's death expressed love and compassion and shared my pain. But this was my first experience of people sharing *memories* and of a man who'd been much respected. It was humbling to recognise that my knowledge of him was limited by my lifetime and had been distorted by his mental illness and more recent physical weakness.

It was true that, when he was well enough to go out, people would see a kind and caring gentleman, a loving and committed father proud of his children, and a trustworthy friend always ready to listen, sympathise and offer prayer. At his best he was cheerful and a sparkling conversationalist, full of wit and humour yet capable of shrewd judgements and wise reflections. He had had a particularly good bedside manner – a blend of compassion, gentleness, comfort and uplifting words – his own battles with ill health giving him an insight and sensitivity that made people feel cherished. Wherever he went he inspired appreciation and affection.

Of course I saw all this too and treasured him for it. But in some ways perhaps I was too close. Sadly life at home was sometimes very different. The illness deprived him of the ability to reach out to others, so robbing him (and them) of the expression of the amazing 'people' qualities I've just described – perhaps his greatest gifts.

I saw the negativity and anxiety that held him captive. I saw the self-doubt, self-preoccupation and depression that tormented him. I saw how all this curtailed his social life, imprisoning him at home, cutting him off from those who he was so gifted to encourage and delight.

This engendered another roller coaster of emotions. The letters and cards reminded me that it wasn't just that little bundle of skin and bones that was no more. The reality was that we'd lost a vibrant human being. But this loss had taken place almost imperceptibly over many many years. That man I was reading about had actually gone long ago and I'd barely known him. I caught a glimpse of a life that had been much fuller and richer than the little I'd seen and the loss seemed greater.

Busyness carried me through those early days. I had a funeral to plan. I reread Psalm 23, remembering how Dad had been comforted by the familiar words as I recited it that last night before he died. I selected from it these words for the cover of the service sheet:

> '*Surely goodness and mercy shall follow me all the days of my life: and I will dwell in the house of the Lord forever.*'
>
> (King James Version)

I decided to read the psalm as part of the service. I pored over hymn books, trying to recall Dad's favourites and wished I'd asked him way ahead of time. I finally chose three uplifting hymns – 'How Great Thou Art', 'In Heavenly Love Abiding' and 'Thine be the Glory'. They were all hymns I knew he'd liked and would be familiar to most of those attending. Richard was to read 2 Timothy 4:6-8.

Richard and I had wanted to offer our children the opportunity to attend despite the fact that Dad's deterioration had distanced them in recent months. Richard asked each child individually and each chose to be there. No doubt our own experiences of exclusion from our mum's funeral influenced our willingness to include them.

I contrasted Dad's funeral with Michael's funeral four years before. Would going to their Grandad's funeral help reinstate the concept of death as being a natural progression after a long life? Most grandchildren at some stage grieve for their grandparents. I mused that a more distant relationship could be a less intense introduction to the concept of death.

Catherine had had very little involvement with her Grandad. Since her birth he'd found it difficult to have a baby or toddler around. There had been no equivalent of the 'Do you want to see a fishy?' interaction that Jonathan had known. I didn't think Catherine really knew who he was and wasn't at an age to find the service meaningful. In the end I judged it better to leave her with friends. That way I could give myself more fully to the service.

Miriam's father (Richard's father-in-law) offered to play the organ. While waiting for the service to start, the words on the front of the service sheet,

'*Surely goodness and mercy shall follow me all the days of my life: and I will dwell in the house of the Lord forever*' prompted him to play a song tune based on these words.

It was beautiful – a delightful reminder of the best of all that Dad had known in life. It carried too the promise that he was now experiencing fullness of life with his God, feasting at the table God had prepared for him. In fact the whole service was lovely.

The funeral and wake were a welcome opportunity to reconnect with friends and relatives who lived at a distance. I was touched again by their respect and appreciation for my father. Sharing recollections seemed a fitting way to bring some conclusion to his life. There were also the oft-repeated expressions of gratitude that he was spared further suffering. All in all it was a joyful occasion with the shared belief that he was now in a much better place.

Was I beginning to cope better with grief? Or was it easier after all in that he was old? Certainly it was less agonising than the deaths of my mother as a child and of Michael and the baby I miscarried. But there were aspects that I still found difficult.

With Michael's death everyone knew of our grief. My dad's death was more hidden. I'd learnt from Michael's death that it was important to talk and not to let a barrier of silence grow between me and my friends. But this time, apart from the really close friends with whom we'd left the children at those final visits, few people knew. News hadn't travelled as it had with Michael's death and I didn't know who knew or whether to talk about it. There was no obvious way of bringing it into the conversation.

My natural reserve coupled with a desire to protect people from unnecessary embarrassment caused me to keep the knowledge to myself in many situations. I felt almost apologetic. Weren't there already too many deaths in my life? Surely people would want to relate to me in other ways? Might I be in danger of finding my identity as a bereaved person? Would it be a self-pity trip?

It was only later that I realised my mistake. It would have been so much more helpful to make myself vulnerable and share my needs. In fact it created a secret inner world – like a small hidden room where my emotions bounced off one wall to another, underlining the loneliness of grief.

Another difficulty was that a garage conversion had been planned. Friends were to carry out this work for us. This was the last thing I wanted. Knowing that my father had left me money I wanted to wait and move house later and perhaps have room for some of my father's furniture.

Malcolm, however, felt we'd made a commitment to have the work done and we should honour it. But I didn't enjoy the noise and endless decisions at a time when there was my father's bungalow and possessions to clear. In retrospect it would have been good to talk more openly with our friends and discover whether it would have suited them to delay the work a little longer.

Clearing the bungalow brought back many memories as we encountered items that had been part of our childhood. Dad had parted with so little when he moved from our family home to the bungalow. In fact so many ornaments and little items as well as furniture brought back recollections of my mum. I would have liked to keep more but we had no storage space.

Parting with these possessions symbolised a break-up of the past – reminiscences of a childhood which could never be recaptured. It underlined that we were no longer children. Richard and I each had three children and had been caring for Dad for years. Yet I found a sense of vulnerability in acknowledging that I was an orphan. We were truly adults – the next generation.

I became aware of a grief for my mum being stirred in all this. Perhaps losing a second parent automatically touches on the grief for the first. But it felt inappropriate. These were emotions that should have been neatly compartmentalised and processed by now, I reasoned. It was a new season. But grief is like a wind that recognises no boundaries. It can scoop up last year's autumn's leaves and fling them mercilessly and whimsically in all directions. I felt battered and bewildered.

Only four months after my father's death I discovered I was pregnant (with Lizzy). This came in the midst of the building work and was a big surprise. I was aware that it was early days

in the grieving process. Having become aware that, even in the
womb, a baby can be sensitive to the mother's emotions, I asked
God to deal with any grief still inside me that could harm my
unborn baby. That very night I had an amazing dream.

I dreamed I was visiting Dad in the nursing home where he'd
lain so ill on the bed. I walked in, taking a careful look. He looked
awful. Was he alive?

Then he opened his eyes and smiled. The colour rushed back into
his face. He looked younger and more relaxed. 'I feel so much better,'
he said. 'You *do* look better,' I agreed. Then to my amazement he got
out of bed and walked easily across the room to joke with the nurses
and have a cup of tea with them.

At this point in my dream the room expanded to become a
largish hall. Only Malcolm and the children had originally come
with me to see Dad but now the room began to fill with people.
My brother and all his family were there. My aunt, Dad's sister,
was there with all six of her children and their families. Many
friends and acquaintances were there. But there was no sense of
crowding or hustle and bustle. It was a relaxed friendly occasion
with a warm peaceful atmosphere – and Dad at the centre of
it all.

Food was being passed around – fantastic party food. Malcolm
was taking photos of family groups. It was like a wedding –
the same sense of joy and excitement and promise of good
things to come. Music was playing and there was a display of
indoor fireworks.

Then a huge chocolate cake was wheeled in. Dad was poised
holding the knife and photographed as he prepared to cut it. It
appeared to round off a lovely occasion. But there was a surprise
grand finale. Petals in pastel colours rained from the ceiling,
floating gently and falling on everyone like confetti. Everyone
gasped in wonder and delight.

At this point I woke up. I came to consciousness with bitter
disappointment with the thought 'But Dad's died. That can't really
happen.' Then straightaway it seemed God corrected me, 'No, you
don't understand. This is my way of saying, "Welcome home!"'

A delicious wave of peace engulfed me. I was so happy to know that Dad was enjoying all this. He was so obviously in his element – thoroughly appreciating it all! It seemed, as far as Dad was concerned, there was no sense of being parted from us. We were together in spirit.

This dream was an enormous help to me. I recollected that at Michael's death I'd 'seen' Michael in the arms of Jesus smiling. It seemed that with my father, too, God wanted me to focus on where Dad was now and his complete enjoyment of the whole scene. It was a picture of celebration and one that has been meaningful in connection with others who've died.

Lizzy was actually born on February 13th – the day before the anniversary of my father's death. She was our fourth child (fifth including Michael) – our third daughter. I was glad she had her own day. Her birthday would be distinctive. It wouldn't be confused with Valentine's Day nor overshadowed by my father's death. In fact the whole pregnancy was an anticipation of life – a reminder that life carries on and with it new hope.

I was sad that Dad would never know this grandchild. But then he'd never really known Catherine. It was time for him to move on. The dream promised a sense of family that not even death could sever. Most of all it was a reminder to me to rejoice in Dad's new life. My loss was less significant in the light of his joy.

What helped?

- The gradual awareness that I'd already lost the Dad I'd known – the intensity of grief was measured into smaller chunks over eighteen months
- The Home warning us that he mightn't have long – this prepared us
- Seeing him shortly before he died which gave me opportunity to say goodbye and read Scripture and pray with him
- Hearing hymns playing in the background, helping underline that he was moving to a new home – this reassured me he was being 'prepared'

🐾 The naturalness of his death – he died in his sleep and of old age

🐾 The happy thought that he was joining Mum on Valentine's Day

🐾 Meeting my brother, Richard, at the Home the next morning, making arrangements for the funeral and sharing responsibilities together

🐾 Composing letters about his death and informing people of the funeral arrangements

🐾 Receiving many letters and cards in response, sharing memories and sharing in our loss and communicating the joy people had experienced in knowing him at his best (these helped fill in my rather sketchy memories from my childhood and early adulthood)

🐾 The dream reassuring me of Dad's happiness – it's focus on celebration and the sense of being together as family

What didn't help?

◊ Dad's inability to speak – limiting communication

◊ My reticence in acknowledging to him that he was dying, that I was saying goodbye and that I might not see him again

◊ The realisation that I was now an orphan – this brought back memories of my mum and unresolved grief for her

◊ The timing of the garage conversion – it began at a time when I didn't want noise, intrusion and the constant need for decisions

What could help?

🐾 Encouraging medical staff to inform when they believe the end is near, while acknowledging this can be difficult in practice. (Even specialists find it difficult to judge and are cautious lest they get it wrong and upset people, but perhaps inviting an honest evaluation may help.)

🦶 Saying goodbye – acknowledging to the dying person that it might not be the last visit but explaining that you were treating it as if it might be

🦶 Overcoming embarrassment so not inhibited in speaking openly, praying, sharing Scripture (if this would be appreciated by the dying person)

🦶 Talking honestly about things you want to share ahead of time before restricted by communication difficulties – e.g. saying goodbyes, gratitude, sharing memories, funeral wishes etc.

🦶 Playing of music that is comforting to the dying person

🦶 Letters and cards sharing memories

🦶 Talking openly with family members who are sharing in grieving

🦶 Focusing on the positive – e.g. the joy of those entering into the presence of God, keeping grief in context

5 Matthew – My Son's Friend

Matthew was Jonathan's best friend. They'd known each other as long as they could remember. From the time Jonathan was two Matthew had come to every birthday party.

They started school together and somehow as parents we'd bought identical blue-grey anoraks, so they looked like twins. In fact there were times when it was hard to separate them and to get Jonathan home. They'd been in the same class at school till they were twelve. It was a very easy-going relationship – each accepted and understood by the other.

As families too we were close. Tim and Jill (Matthew's parents) were very good friends of ours. Their daughter, Hannah, was just a year younger than our daughter, Rachel. Their youngest daughter, Naomi, was in age between our two youngest daughters, Catherine and Lizzy. So it was easy for us to spend time together because everyone had a friend and was happy!

When Jonathan and Matthew were thirteen we moved six miles away from Cobham to Great Bookham near Leatherhead – still in Surrey. We made sure that the boys had opportunity to meet up. Jonathan went to Matthew's to stay every other weekend. They played football and computer games. Jonathan often stayed overnight and they chatted till late. Jonathan felt he could talk to Matthew about anything, confident that Matthew wouldn't tell anyone else. Then they would sometimes cycle over to Bookham together to spend the next day at our house.

Matthew and Jonathan, now fourteen, were actively involved in the life of the church. Each had a strong faith but Matthew seemed marked out as a future church leader. Already he was sometimes asked to pray in big church gatherings – words expressed simply but full of power.

One evening, chatting with a friend, he declared confidently, 'I'm not afraid of dying. I know where I'm going. And it's going to be great!

Five days later I had a phone call from Stuart. He informed me that Matthew was having trouble breathing and was in hospital. The church was to gather that evening to pray for him. He trailed off with the words, 'But we need a miracle.'

What did this mean? I told Jonathan. He went very quiet. We were both in shock and didn't feel like eating tea. I was eager to go to the church meeting and pray together for Matthew and get everything back to normal.

It was a time when people were experiencing God in fresh ways – sometimes called 'the Toronto blessing'. To accommodate this, the church was gathering together three times a week. Many had been laughing uncontrollably as they were touched by God.

But tonight we walked into a very different atmosphere. There was no laughter. Many people were crying. The tears annoyed me. Surely we were praying for Matthew to recover! This was a time to believe.

A church leader announced the bare facts. Matthew's friend, David, (Stuart and Jayne's eldest son) had rung Matthew that morning while Matthew was still in bed. It was discovered that Matthew wasn't breathing and he'd been rushed to hospital. He was in intensive care on a life support system. There appeared to be no brain activity. Only a miracle could save him.

Then it will have to be a miracle, I reasoned. The alternative was unthinkable. Matthew was an integral part of our family, Tim and Jill's family, our young people, our church, our community. Matthew was strong. These things don't happen to healthy energetic fourteen year olds.

Jonathan wanted to go to the hospital. 'Maybe you can see Matthew tomorrow,' I said. 'Matthew is dead,' he retorted. The stark words confronted me from a chasm between us. I couldn't receive them. I couldn't bear for it to be true. How could my son lose a brother and now a best friend? How could my close friends lose their son?

Next day Jonathan, along with David and other friends were taken to the hospital. Hearing that the nurses were praying for Matthew, some began to hope for recovery. Prayer wasn't a superstition for these young people and their theology didn't include praying for the dead. To pray meant to hope.

But Tim and Jill took them into a side room to talk. They wanted the boys to understand that this was not just visiting a friend in hospital. They wanted them to be clear that Matthew had died and this was 'goodbye'.

I'd sent a note with Jonathan to Tim and Jill. I longed to be with them! What agony they must be going through! But would I be in the way?

We were urged to come quickly. The situation needed to be brought to a conclusion. It sounded as if the life support machine was soon to be switched off. But surely it hadn't really come to this!

We found a scene of great peace. Tim and Jill seemed supernaturally calm and accepting. Despite the tubes and apparatus Matthew looked well. There was colour in his face. His chest was rising and falling. He could have been asleep.

Yet, somehow he was absent. Instead I could see him energetically riding his bike – exploring heaven. Was this a picture from God?

It was like giving a friend a final goodbye wave, only to realise he's already finished waving and has turned away. Matthew had moved on. I was confusingly confident he was enjoying a new life.

But emotionally I was in limbo. Still numb with shock it felt like trying to complete a jigsaw with most of the pieces missing. My mind was still grappling with the impossibility of a healthy teenager suddenly dying in his bed.

We returned home and collected Catherine and Lizzy. Again we read together 'What Happens when we Die?' – the same book that we'd found so helpful after Michael's death. Catherine was six – only a few months younger than Jonathan had been when we'd read it then. The memories of Michael came flooding back. We knew that Matthew's death too would impact us deeply as a family.

But it was to Tim and Jill that our hearts went out. How could it be? … their firstborn child … their only son … such little warning?

The next day I suggested Jonathan stay home from school. But he wanted to go. He thought his friends would be supportive. So I let him.

His friends were very kind. His History lesson was fine. But Biology was a lesson about how all living things need water. It hit Jonathan afresh that Matthew would never again drink water. Jonathan ran from the room crying.

Another friend was also struggling. She too had left her lesson. It was good to have each other – a comfort to share their grief. They were given permission to leave school so they joined other young people in a home in Cobham.

It was a sombre gathering. Most were aged only fourteen and were still in shock. The room filled up as, one by one, they all gave up on school until there were twenty of them. It was reassuring that others were grieving too and would be there to share the journey.

A church leader joined them. They read the Bible together. Someone mispronounced a word. They began to laugh. Was it because their emotions were heightened? They just couldn't get through reading the passage from the Bible. It seemed extraordinary to laugh in the midst of grief but it was healing. Perhaps too, despite the huge impact of Matthew's death, there was a realisation that life would go on.

Both Jonathan and Rachel were brought face to face once more with their own mortality. Death could happen at any time – not just in old age. It could strike without warning. They were at an age when this made a big impact.

Rachel too was in tears at school. A teacher, baffled, questioned her harshly, 'Why are *you* crying? It's not *your* friend who's died?

How could the death of a friend of her brother's affect her so deeply? Evidently such closeness between families was outside this teacher's experience.

We were all hurting. We needed extra love and understanding. I felt aggrieved that my daughter was being told off for crying, simply because it wasn't *her* friend who had died. Having suffered so much from suppressing my emotions as a child, I was relieved that my children *could* cry to release their grief. Rachel rarely made a fuss at school. I was disappointed that instead of compassion she was receiving rebuke.

I wrote a letter to the school, explaining that we were very close as a family to the friend who had died. I also explained that Rachel's little brother had died nearly eight years before – when she was only four. This new loss might well be triggering off more grief from her baby brother. I appealed for gentleness and understanding.

It had been a difficult day for me too. I started to grieve about 36 hours after everyone else – partly because I was late hearing what had happened and partly because I was believing for a miracle. Then I was putting myself in Tim and Jill's shoes and in Jonathan's shoes – trying to imagine what they must be feeling as well as dealing with my own grief.

Today was Tim's birthday. How could he enjoy a birthday when he'd lost his son? What was there to celebrate?

As I changed Lizzy's nappy I thought of all the baby care that Jill had given Matthew – all those nappy changes … all that feeding. For 14 years Jill had sacrificially poured love and care into him to make him the young man he'd become –taller than her and so mature. She'd been so proud of him. And now he was gone.

Tim, too, had enjoyed a very close relationship with Matthew. He'd loved watching Matthew as a young child in the garden with the rabbits and splashing about in the paddling pool. As Matthew grew older they shopped for clothes together. And then there was Romania… Matthew had visited children in a home there twice. The plight of the children had made a big impact on them both. Matthew had wanted to talk to them about God and was even learning their language in order to communicate better with them. So many of his sentences began with the phrase, 'When I was in Romania...' It had become a standing joke. But never again would Tim hear those words from him.

How I longed to ease the pain for them! I was overcome by grief but trying not to cry in front of my little ones. I felt sick to my stomach with emotion I didn't know how to express. Slowly it dawned on me that however much I wanted to carry the grief Tim and Jill and Jonathan had to bear, I couldn't grieve on their behalf. I could only deal with my own pain.

It was as if I was trying to take on the offence against them. I was trying to feel for them. I was imagining their loss and trying to carry a load that wasn't mine. God had met me in my own grief for Michael. He'd met me in a different way in my grief over the miscarriage. But something bizarre was operating here. In trying to put myself in Tim and Jill's shoes and in Jonathan's shoes, I was imagining a grief unrelieved by the grace of God. I realised identification has limited usefulness. Trying to carry their grief would help them no more than I'd helped my father when I'd tried to share his depression.

It was hard to let it go. I felt almost guilty. Wasn't it heartless to dismiss it? Yet it seemed a denial of the grace of God to hold on to it. Little by little I learnt to feel only my own grief. That was bad enough.

How healing it was to spend time with Tim and Jill that evening! Hearing the details of their story filled in huge gaps in the sketchy outline I'd been given. Somehow the simple recounting of the facts satisfied an emotional longing. Where I'd felt distanced by lack of information, I now found myself being connected and feeling included.

Tim and Hannah had gone to school that fateful morning. Matthew had an INSET day so he was sleeping in. When David rang to speak to Matthew, Jill had tried to wake him, pushing and pulling his bare shoulder. She'd cried, 'He's not breathing! Get

Jayne quick.' (Stuart and Jayne and their family lived just a few doors down the road.)

Jill had rung 999. Stuart and Jayne had got Matthew's body to the floor and attempted to resuscitate him.

When the ambulance arrived, three men carried Matthew down in a reclining chair with an oxygen mask. Jill grabbed some phone numbers and followed Matthew into the ambulance. The ambulance men were pumping Matthew's heart while Jill held his hand.

They sped off to Epsom hospital, siren wailing. They hurtled along roads that were so familiar and held such significant memories. How could it be that they were travelling them in this horrific way?

At the hospital Jill was shown into an office near the Accident and Emergency waiting room. A cup of tea was brought. Nine doctors were working on Matthew in the room next door. Why were they getting no brain reaction?

Tim was summoned to Epsom Hospital. This was the third serious phone call in five days. On Saturday Jill had narrowly escaped death in a car crash. Soon after that his father had died. But now all this was eclipsed by the news of his son. Jill informed him 'He's still alive. But they can't find any brain activity. But the doctors don't have the last word. God is his doctor.' Jill was calm and surprisingly strong – her emotions on hold.

The next little while was a blur of doctors, nurses and cups of tea. Jill recalled the events of the previous day. That too had been an INSET day so she had been with Matthew all day for an annual appointment with their podiatrist. Matthew had helped with directions and chatted about how he'd like to learn to drive this car.

Before going to bed Jill had kissed each of her sleeping children, praying over them as usual. There had been nothing abnormal with Matthew. What could have happened?

Now in intensive care Matthew was hooked up to some noisy machines. One helped him breathe. Sometimes the rhythm changed frighteningly.

Hannah, aged eleven, came to visit. She was alarmed to see her brother connected to so many tubes. Tim and Jill reassured her – perhaps too well, Jill reflected.

For Tim and Jill it was a long night. The armchairs in their room nearby didn't make good beds. Each time they nodded off they were awakened by the noise of staff using the lifts just outside and doors banging. Then they would be struck afresh with the awful realisation of why they were there.

More and more tests were carried out. None showed any brain activity. The medical diagnosis was an arteriovenous malformation.

Apparently the brain had not formed correctly. There had been nothing to indicate this previously but some capillaries running between the arteries and veins were missing. A sudden haemorrhage from the thin vessel walls, like a massive stroke, had resulted in severe brain damage. His heart wouldn't continue to function so the machines were soon to be switched off.

Hannah was brought to the hospital. Tim told her that Matthew had died. She burst into tears. She was stunned… totally unprepared.

Going home in the car, Jill spoke out the same words from Job as I had with Michael – 'The Lord gives and the Lord takes away. Blessed be the name of the Lord.' It was a declaration of trust but there were many unanswered questions.

Why three life and death issues in six days? They puzzled over the car crash. 'Someone's looking after you,' the police had commented, amazed Jill had survived. The God who had stepped in then could have intervened with Matthew too. It was oddly reassuring.

Listening to Tim and Jill's account, strangely facilitated my grieving. It gave me the substance and immediacy I needed. It became a pathway on which to walk through my own grief.

Despite their intense pain, it was clear that gratitude was a big element of their response. It was encouraging to see how God was supporting them through this. They'd been touched by the kindness of the medical staff. Jill had unusually been allowed to accompany Matthew in the ambulance and they'd been treated with great consideration.

The church family too had been such a strength. Tim and Jill appreciated the cards they'd already received, expressing such delightful things about Matthew. One from a young friend of Matthew's said, 'He was so easy to talk to when I felt down. Such a good listener and so understanding…Just looking at him you saw strength, compassion and confidence radiating from him … Reliable and caring. He never seemed embarrassed about standing up for his God.'

The cards and letters were so precious and helpful and reminded them that they weren't alone in their grief. Everyone had lost Matthew. But perhaps Tim and Jill were most thankful that Matthew wasn't afraid of death – that he knew where he was going and that one day they would see him again.

It was good for Rachel and Hannah to spend the evening together. They had lost brothers very different in age but few other friends had experienced any bereavement. Together they could share a little of their grief.

The next day, Saturday, David came over to Bookham to have lunch with us and to spend time with Jonathan. They'd both been struck severely. Both had lost their best friend. Jonathan was aware that the move to Bookham, though a wrench at the time, had softened the blow a little. He hadn't seen Matthew every day. There had been a separation already. What agony it was for David, living just a few doors along in the same road and attending the same school! And then there were the joint family holidays that David had spent with Matthew!

Next day was the Sunday church gathering. Jonathan normally sat with Matthew – along with the other young people. What a hole Matthew's absence would leave! As people gathered, Matthew was always so welcoming. During the worship he'd operated the overhead projector to display the words for us to sing. He'd involved himself practically wherever he could be useful.

But it wasn't just the things that he did. Matthew was an integral part of the church and emanated confidence in God. He'd been an inspiration to everyone. Jonathan's card for Tim and Jill closed with these words,

> *'... Matthew acted like there was purpose in life, and threw himself into whatever he was doing wholeheartedly. He was happy. His happiness encouraged us all in our faith, because we felt he'd seen something that made life worth living and together we sought to find God in the most real ways possible.'*

The church gathering was an opportunity to express our grief together. I was glad to receive prayer from a friend. I wanted to linger there afterwards – to enjoy the togetherness. The corporate sharing of grief was such a comfort.

I was still hankering after this the next day. I woke at 4.00am and was unable to sleep again. I felt so cut off in Bookham. Never good at crying I was desperate to release my grief through talking. That was so much easier with Michael's death. Everyone had come to *me* and I could talk it through with them again and again and again and receive their love and prayers that were so healing.

I wanted to talk *this* through with everyone but there was no one to talk to. I wanted to receive love and prayer but there was no one to give it. When I'd felt lonely in Bookham in the past I'd rung Jill or Jayne. How could I ring either of them now? Jayne was busy caring for Jill, answering the phone, looking after Tim and Jill's girls. Then I felt guilty. How could I be selfishly thinking of *my* needs when for Tim and Jill it must be so much worse? What was my grief in comparison with Jill's?

It was a time to be together and draw strength from one another. But I was without a car and there was no direct bus. Then who would I see anyway? Lizzy was only two so I was limited in the help I could give – I would be more of an encumbrance. Finally I plucked up courage to ring another friend. Lifts were arranged and I gratefully met up with others who were feeling like me.

Such relief! It was so good to share our questions, our memories and our grief together.

Several young people, including Jonathan, were asked to contribute at Matthew's Thanksgiving Service. The day began with pouring rain. Was heaven itself crying with us?

Seven hundred people attended the service – relatives, many friends and a few pupils. Jill dreaded her daughter, Naomi, (who was only three) asking what was in the box! But she didn't.

It was a time to rejoice in all God had given in Matthew and in all Matthew was enjoying with God. It was an extraordinary event, expressing overwhelming appreciation for Matthew. But what a shame he hadn't had that encouragement in life! I resolved to value people more while they were alive – to live each day grateful for them in case there's no tomorrow.

It was early December. We sang a new song telling the Christmas story from Mary's perspective – looking ahead to the day she would lose her son. Poignant and so haunting, it seemed to encapsulate this whole grief experience. There was such a wonderful sense of celebration of all Matthew had meant to so many. Yet every delightful memory was tinged with the pain of loss.

Perhaps, too, for me it brought back memories of Michael – *my* baby born at Christmas. I'd identified so strongly with Mary. I remembered the sense at his birth that there was something very special about him. Then too I'd known the bittersweet mingling of the joy of new life and the pain of death so soon – symbolised by the juxtaposition of new baby cards with sympathy cards. Was this why I was feeling Matthew's death so acutely?

The next day we went to the crematorium. The Thanksgiving had been bittersweet. This was just bitter. It was dark and so cold. In contrast to the huge number at the Thanksgiving it was a small group at the Crematorium. It underlined the intimacy of grief. It was so very gruelling and heart-rending.

I reflected on the power of emotions. Were they part of the richness of life? We're glad to experience intense joy. To feel joy fully do we need also to suffer grief fully?

Again our hearts went out to Tim and Jill. They'd requested that, rather than flowers, donations be made to help the children in Romania. We looked together at the few special flowers that had been sent and the cards that accompanied them – so touching. Tim's heaving sobs were agonising to witness. I instinctively put my arm round Jill. Then I felt awkward and self-conscious. Was my gesture an intrusion? Who was I to presume to comfort? Yet how I longed to ease their pain! I felt so helpless.

How was Jonathan doing? What did it mean to him at fourteen to have his best friend die? Some of his friends had never faced death before – not even of a grandparent. Losing Michael at seven and then his Grandad at eleven had prepared him a little. He had a confidence in God and knew Matthew was in heaven.

But those first days, weeks and months were very hard. Yes life would go on but it was depressing… pointless. Yet he found a special bond grew with those who shared his beliefs and talked openly of their grief and their hope that they would meet again.

For many years Jonathan continued to dream of Matthew. They were nearly always playing football and chatting. Matthew was usually the same age as at his death – Jonathan sometimes older. They were aware of a gap between them as if one of them had been abroad for a long time and there was a lot to catch up on. Each time he woke he cried afresh – struck again by the agony of loss. Was this a reprocessing of his grief? Did he need to recognise what this loss meant to him at his current age?

After several years of this torment, Jonathan made a decision. Why not be grateful that at least he had the chance to be with Matthew in his dreams? So he resolved to be positive – to be glad when he dreamed of Matthew. He decided to respond with these thoughts – 'I've got a chance to see him again – this is something to enjoy – I can remember him as he was. Yes – I still feel I've lost a close friend – but I've got him as a friend in my dreams.' Since making this choice, Jonathan reflected he was less troubled by these dreams.

At least his grief over Matthew was very clean and uncomplicated. There was no guilt – nothing had tarnished the relationship. He contrasted it with a relationship break-up. That could be hurtful, often involving endless heart-searching, regret and blame or self-blame. But, as it was, all his memories of Matthew were only good and wholesome.

Had his life been changed? Undoubtedly! At an impressionable age he'd been forced to think about the transience of life and yet its eternal significance. It inspired him to want his own life to be meaningful. Matthew's certainty about heaven and how good it was had challenged Jonathan to declare the same words to *his* friends, 'I know where I'm going. And it's going to be great!'

Matthew's sister, Hannah, gathered the young people together for a special meal 10 years after his death. It was a time to remember Matthew and consider how his life had touched them all. He'd influenced their lives with a power that many longer lives had not. He'd wanted his life to count and it had been more significant than he'd known. In his own way he *had* been a leader. They were aware too that his death as well as his life had had a huge impact.

One special story was told by Philip Jinadu, who'd been a leader of the young people and an evangelist. At Spring Harvest (a large Christian conference), over three years after Matthew's death, he'd spoken to the 12-14 year olds about Matthew. He told them how, a few days before his death, Matthew had said he wasn't afraid of dying – he was looking forward to heaven.

Philip called for a response. Who wanted to be that confident about what would happen when they died? Who wanted to follow Jesus? There was a huge surge of movement. The band thought everyone was leaving! But 73 young people made a first-time commitment – a declaration that they wanted to have that certainty.

The next day after a worship meeting a girl about Matthew's age was watching some sport and collapsed. Twenty minutes later she was declared dead. This tragedy underlined Philip's story. Death could happen at any time. Were they ready? A further wave of young people also gave their lives to Jesus for the first time. In all about a hundred young people responded.

Matthew's life and death had been an inspiration and a challenge to everyone who'd known him. But he'd also influenced many who simply heard his story. As for me… I'd been impacted more than I knew…

What helped?

For all of us (our family and the church)

- Matthew's faith and confidence that he was going to heaven and it would be great

- Certainty that we would see Matthew again

- Having good memories of Matthew

- Opportunity to say goodbye to Matthew in hospital (even though he'd already died)

- Support of friends who were also grieving for Matthew

For us as a family

- Our move to Bookham had already distanced Jonathan a little from Matthew

- Reading as a family 'What Happens when we Die?'

- Previous experiences of loss had prepared us to some extent

- Hearing the details of what had happened to Matthew

- Jonathan – Choosing to be glad when he dreamed of Matthew

For the young people

- Being a close-knit group who could support one another – knowing others were grieving too and understood their pain

- Church leader supporting the young people – leading them in reading from the Bible

- Laughing even when it seemed incongruous

What didn't help

For me

◊ Trying to grieve for other people – or at least imagining only the negative aspects of what they were feeling

◊ Being cut off geographically from others who were grieving and from whom I could receive support

◊ Initially having very little information on what had happened

For Rachel

◊ Unsympathetic teacher

6 *More about Mum*

Matthew's death came at a time when I already felt emotionally vulnerable. My self-image was very low. At the root of this was a lack of identity.

Life was busy with four children. Jonathan was fourteen, Rachel was twelve, Catherine was six and Lizzy was two and a half. I regarded my inability to keep the house clean and tidy as proof of my personal incompetence. I used my job list like a whip to chastise myself. Though I worked hard, I ended every day with a sense of failure.

In this emotional state Matthew's death hit me hard. Ten days later I was starting to suspect that there was another dimension to the grief. I reflected on this in my journal.

Saturday 10th December 1994

> (the day after the service at the crematorium)

> *'If there's more grief from Michael (rather than Matthew) to come out, I don't know what to do about it. I don't want to be looking for something which isn't there...Maybe there's a sense in which you always grieve.*

> *In some ways I feel my grief from Michael is very clean. But I'm less sure about the grief from my mum, which I handled all wrongly at the time and have had to patch up bit by bit since and there may still be some weak areas.'*

Little did I realise what an understatement that was and how much grief over my mum's death I still had to deal with – at that time and over the next fourteen years! All I knew was that it was a time to listen to my inner self and bring it to God. I took refuge in the fact that he knew me through and through, having put me together in my mum's womb.

Sunday 18th December 1994

> 'As God is stirring things up, I can say to him, "Yes. I yield. I invite you in to touch these deeper areas of my life." God is going to come in deeper and breathe into the very fabric of my life and emotions – deeper than he ever has before – into this great area of grief.
>
> So I yield to you, Father. I bring all this grief to you. I invite you to come deep inside and breathe your healing love into those areas of pain.'

I saw a picture of a well – clear water at the top but it was very very deep and right at the very bottom it wasn't clear – there was muck that had been there for years. But God was reaching down into the well with a long stick.

It seemed that Matthew's death was reawakening agonising emotions that had been there a long time – an incapacitating sense of desolation and loneliness. I cried out to God, 'It's all so painful. I feel like stuff from my mum's death is being stirred up now – areas of grief that go very deep. I feel so desperate and so miserable.'

Was God using Matthew's death to reach the grief I'd locked away? Their deaths had even occurred at the same time of year. Matthew's death was 30th November and my mum's 6th December. Could it be that God was working at a deeper level than I could have coped with before? How long would it take to release pain that had been locked up for so many years?

God was bringing back feeling. It was like a leg with pins and needles. It was reminiscent of the phase when you would almost rather be numb again than face the acute discomfort of reawakened sensation.

I cried out again,

> *'Father, I need your comfort. I invite you into everything I'm feeling. I allow the pain to surface and I choose to receive your love to heal. Thank you that you know the way through this grief. You will hold my hand and take me through it step by step.*

Psalm 142:6-7

⁶Listen to my cry,
for I am in desperate need;
rescue me from those who pursue me,
> *(especially guilt, regret and disappointment)*
for they are too strong for me.
⁷Set me free from my prison,
that I may praise your name.'

A few days later I woke with the thought, 'But I didn't really say goodbye...' I've learnt to listen to these early morning insights so I pondered further. No – I didn't say goodbye to Matthew while alive and I didn't say goodbye to Michael while alive. But I'd said goodbye to both of them in death.

But my mum? No goodbye of any sort – alive or dead. I didn't know she was so ill. I didn't see her at the end. I wasn't allowed at the funeral. In fact I had a feeling of being excluded from everything. Was that my childish perspective? Or was I really shut out by well-meaning adults?

I recollected how healing it had been to talk to Tim and Jill and hear the story of Matthew's death. Perhaps the geographical distance and lack of communication resonated with the distancing and exclusion I'd experienced in my childhood. There was the same awkwardness and embarrassment about asking questions – the anxiety that I might be an intrusion.

After my mum's death I hadn't wanted to upset people. Later it was easier to pull a curtain over all that had happened and blank it from my consciousness. But now these questions were surfacing again.

How long had she been ill? ...Was she expected to die? ...What had happened at the end? ...Why didn't we go to the funeral? ... What did my brother know about it? ...How did he feel?

I rang Richard, knowing these were questions I should have asked years before! He was out but I spoke to my sister-in-law, Miriam, asking if Richard would write down his recollections of that time. I asked the same of Aunty Ruby.

I began to wonder if suppressed grief was at the root of the issues with my self-image and with guilt, resentment and self-pity, as well as my difficulties in the home. It could explain a lot. My mind felt muddled – everyday life was extremely difficult. I couldn't think about food. In fact everything felt burdensome.

Again I cried out in my journal,

"O Lord, hear my prayer,
listen to my cry for mercy;
in your faithfulness and righteousness
come to my relief.'

(Psalm 143:1)

I look to you to deal with all these areas. Just show
me how to respond to you a step at a time and give
me grace to make that right response.

'Rescue me from my enemies, O Lord,
for I hide myself in you.'"

(Psalm 143:9)

It was nearly Christmas. Grief had taken over and I still hadn't bought a Christmas present for Malcolm. I left the younger children with the older ones so I could shop without a pushchair and more easily battle through the crowds. I also needed some space for me – space to grieve.

But it was also excruciating. The bus times had changed so I had to wait for 40 minutes. I'd been used to keeping myself busy at home. With four children there was always plenty of work. But for once there was nothing I could do but stand at the bus stop and wait for my bus. I couldn't escape. There was no respite from the pain.

Yet it was a space for God. It was an encounter with him. I was conscious of God holding me in this grief – as I stood there at the bus stop … and also as a child and through all my life. He'd watched over me with gentleness and compassion and had grieved with me. He'd given me Aunty Ruby and used all the experiences in my life to open me up to him.

I yielded the grief to him again. I cried out for complete healing. I remembered how he'd shown me how to grieve for Michael and I trusted him to help me apply what I'd learnt then to this suppressed grief.

I remembered how talking had been such a key then. I knew I should talk about my Mum and how I felt. But it wasn't so easy when it was all so long ago and no one around me had known her. I prayed that Richard and Aunty Ruby would write letters that would open up opportunities to talk.

Finally the bus arrived but, in my absent-minded condition, I had no cash. The bus driver had compassion on me and let me on anyway and took me to Guildford. In my contemplative state of mind it felt like a reflection of God's heart – taking me on a journey for which I didn't have the resources. I felt so inadequate to take this journey back to the grief of my childhood.

I wasn't in the mood for shopping. It aggrieved me to see the world rushing by in its crazy spending spree oblivious of the torture I was enduring! What was the point of it all? Material things had lost their appeal – they seemed too transient – too superficial – too trivial. But I bought a present and returned home as soon as I could.

A few days after Christmas I was delighted to receive a typewritten letter from Richard, recalling the time around Mum's death.

29th December 1994

Dear Barbara,

>   *... I spent the evening of Wednesday*
> *6 December 1961 doing my homework. When Dad*
> *arrived back from Epsom hospital that evening, I*
> *was sitting on the armchair on the right-hand side*
> *of the fireplace in the dining room, still doing my*
> *English literature homework.*
>
>   *Dad came in and broke the news, 'Mummy has*
> *gone to be with Jesus.'*
>
>   *The news came as a total shock ... I was totally*
> *unprepared. Each previous time Mum had gone*
> *into hospital, she had come out after a few weeks,*
> *and had resumed normal life. I had been expecting*
> *the same thing to happen again. I know Dad had*
> *explained that Mum was very ill, but I had not*
> *taken it in.*
>
>   *... I asked what she had died of. Dad replied*
> *with a long word that meant nothing to me. ...*
> *Auntie Ruby was staying with us at the time. Dad*
> *said Auntie Ruby was with Mum when she died.*
> *The hospital had phoned Dad, but Mum had died*
> *before he arrived.*
>
>   *I was soon aware that Mum had died of cancer*
> *and an infection. We had not been allowed to*
> *visit her in the hospital ... children simply weren't*
> *allowed to visit patients in hospital. You may*
> *remember that, one day, Dad took us to the*
> *hospital. We waved to Mum through the window of*

her room, and used the Lexicon cards to spell out one or two messages.

Dad also told me how Mum died. For some time, she had been lying on her right hand side (to minimise the strain on her heart). She was feeling stiff and sore, and asked to be turned. The nurse turned her ... and someone asked Mum, 'How's that?' Mum replied, 'It's lovely' and died. Dad reckoned that she was beginning to see the glories of heaven.

I wanted to attend mum's funeral, but dad said no and I didn't want to argue. Dad said I might find it upsetting.

... Auntie Ruby returned to Somerset within a few days, but returned to Cheam with Auntie Joan for Christmas. They worked hard to lay on a good Christmas for us...

I expected your reaction to be the same as mine, but it wasn't. You clammed up and for twenty years would not talk about her. If Dad or I mentioned her, you would listen to what we said, but would not pursue the conversation.

Dad never really got over Mum's death. His first breakdown was within four years, with a recurrence every six years thereafter. And when he did plan to remarry, it was to someone who looks very similar to Mum.

Auntie Joan came out with an important comment about ten years ago, when I was visiting her and Auntie Ruby. Mum worried how Dad and you and me would manage without her. Until Auntie Joan said this, it had never occurred to me that Mum might have known that she was going to die. I asked Auntie Joan and, yes, Mum did know that she was going to die.

It was not until Dad died, and we found Mum's
death certificate at the bungalow, that I became
aware that her cancer started as breast cancer.
This has important implications for you. There is a
hereditary element in breast cancer...'

The letter concluded with an encouragement to have breast screening.

A lot of this was new to me. At last I had something tangible to talk about and assimilate. How much it would have helped if I'd talked out my grief in the years following Mum's death! I could have slotted my fragmentary memories into a much larger picture. Why hadn't I done so? I started to blame myself. Why had I been so silent?

I rang Aunty Ruby. It was she who revealed that Dad had been very upset when I tried to talk about my mum. Being sensitive I'd soon learnt to keep off the subject. Later it got difficult for me to talk about it at all.

I rang Richard too about his letter and the events surrounding Mum's death. It was healing to talk. I was especially delighted with the details of how she'd died – that she'd caught a glimpse of heaven and saw that it was lovely. It reminded me of the picture I'd had straight after Michael's death – Michael being held in the arms of Jesus. This was what I needed – a focus on her new life. This would have helped me so much in my childhood. Now I felt almost included in the death scene – it was a memory I could share in. It was a 'goodbye' from this world even if not a personal 'goodbye' to me.

I woke the next morning with the thought that the 23rd Psalm had been brought to my attention in every death of a member of my family. I'd learnt it for Girls' Brigade. Now I realised my Mum had actually been dying at the time I'd been memorising,

'though I walk through the valley of the shadow of death, I
will fear no evil: for thou art with me; thy rod and thy staff
they comfort me.'

Was God comforting me that night even though I didn't know of her death till the morning? Was he confirming his presence and reassuring me of his love?

I photocopied Richard's letter to send to Aunty Ruby. Nearly 82 she might find it helpful to have a framework of Richard's memories into which to insert her own. I badly needed filling in on those last three months – September to November. My only memory was the glimpse through the hospital window when we displayed that get well message with the Lexicon cards.

And Richard's letter had raised other questions which I aired in my journal on Thursday 5th January 1995.

> *'Why did no one tell us she was dying? Were they*
> *hoping for a miracle? It's like a conspiracy that we*
> *weren't part of.*
> *I'm sure it was with the best intentions.*
> *I forgive.'*

At least it was an expression of my desire to forgive. It was the first acknowledgement that we could have been better prepared for her death. The reality was that I had to return to this many more times and continue to choose to forgive.

A few days later, my daughter, Rachel (then 12), prayed for me at church. As she did so, I had a sense of God reaching down with a sieve. He was bringing stuff that had been around for years to the surface and starting to remove it. It reminded me of the picture of the well with clean water on the surface but with muck at the bottom that had been there for years. It reassured me – God was starting to clear it out.

Richard had raised the issue of breast screening. I found that, though too young for routine screening, I could be screened if I got a letter from my doctor. Should I go ahead? I didn't want to be governed by fear and be looking for trouble. But I didn't want to be burying my head in the sand and fail to heed the warning of my mum's breast cancer.

I was exactly the same age as my mum had been when she had a breast removed. Catherine was six – the age I'd been at that time and Lizzy was not yet three. Jonathan, now nearly fifteen, and Rachel at twelve still needed me a lot too. I didn't want to be irresponsible. I didn't really believe I would have cancer too, but then I hadn't the absolute assurance of faith that I wouldn't.

It seemed foolish to decline the facilities available today to be checked. But, perhaps even more compelling, was the thought that, after so many years of denial of my mum's illness and death, it seemed a fitting response – an acknowledgement of what had happened. I was facing up to the facts, even if belatedly.

The breast screening showed everything was fine. I was told that, though I was high risk compared to normal (which is 1%), I still have only a 4% chance of developing breast cancer. It was reassuring to be checked and it gave another opportunity to talk about my mum.

Aunty Ruby's letter arrived. It was worth waiting for.

Dear Barbara and Richard,

> *I will try to supplement Richie's story as much as I can … Kathleen first knew she had trouble when Barbara was nearly six and Richard was ten. … Kathleen had a major operation and was in hospital 2-3 weeks …*

> *She was very determined that she was going to be well again. She succeeded very well for the next 18 months to 2 years … We were all very hopeful about the future.*

> *About 18 months later Kathleen began to get pains in her back and about her body. She thought she had rheumatism. She went to a private doctor who told her there was nothing wrong and she tried to believe him. She didn't improve and made an appointment at the hospital, where it was made obvious that the cancer had spread.*

Kathleen asked me to take Barbara for a few weeks while she was in hospital. She had worried about you before because you were going to different people after school and you couldn't remember where you had to go and stood in the road and cried.

I was delighted to have you for that summer ... Kathleen came out of hospital and after a week or two wanted you home. George came down to fetch you on a baking hot day. I was devastated when you went but happy your mother seemed better.

I didn't see a lot of you for the next few weeks, but was in Surrey during the summer holiday. Barbara hadn't found going back to her own school easy, because she ran straight into exams and of course she hadn't covered the same work.

I went to Surrey again in October for the autumn holiday ... they told me Kathleen had to go to hospital again. We were all very upset. I think it was at that stage that we all realised that Kathleen was not going to come through as we had hoped. But as you should realise we had no idea at that stage how long she might be able to fight on.

During the next few days it was decided by Kathleen and George that Barbara should stay at home and not come with me. This was to get her more settled ...

I can't quite remember when Kathleen went back into hospital but she was there on Nov 5th. I sat outside the hospital in the car while someone else visited with George. I wrote a long very personal letter to Kathleen and watched the rockets going up.

When Kathleen was in hospital she asked me to buy and dress a doll in proper school clothes. It had to have long hair like your own. I expect you remember it. She also asked me to do all I could to help you both.

I was up and down to Surrey during that November, and very busy at school too. Kathleen had been moved into a side room, because there was an infection about in the hospital... I was at school on Dec 5th and late morning I had a phone call from George to say that Kathleen was not as well and perhaps I should come... George had told me to come straight up to the hospital.

Kathleen was very poorly but wanted to talk and for us to talk to her ... Next morning early we were back with Kathleen. Sometime during the day George decided he should go back home to tend to various things and to see that you both would be looked after. (By that time he had the housekeeper.)

I stayed with Kathleen who was quiet and peaceful and wanted me to talk. ... as Rich said, Kathleen was turned over and made more comfortable. I had taken her hand again and the nurse had gone to the other side of the room. I expect I must have asked her how she felt, but I know she said, 'It's lovely!' Certainly I felt at the time that she had seen a vision of her future home. With those words her grasp on my hand loosened, her breathing altered and I feel sure she died ...

Early next morning Barbara came into my bed and I took the chance to tell her about her mother's death. She was very quiet about it ... She wanted to know what would happen to her and could she come back to Somerset with me. I told her I would love to have her, but that her Daddy and Richard would need her to stay with them to keep the family together.

George and I took Barbara to school and explained to her teacher what had happened. Barbara told me that the other children were told and they were all kind to her ...

George and I made the usual plans for the funeral. I never knew that Richard wanted to attend, and it was not discussed. Obviously George didn't think you or Barbara should attend a funeral. George's sister and family and the old father came and some other people. Ron came but we persuaded Mother not to come.

I did go home a few days after the funeral because I had no choice. I wasn't allowed more time out of school, and I had Mother to see to. It would have been better if I could have stayed longer. You both needed to talk and be talked to about your mother.

Richard mentions you were not allowed to visit your mother in hospital. This was hospital ruling at that time.

He also feels that you both should have been told that your mother would die – but when you should have been told I don't know. Kathleen could well have come out of hospital again. We did not know how soon death would come. I think the infection in the hospital probably hastened the end.

I think you must ask me anything else you want to know, and I will help if I can.

With love from
Aunty Ruby

Life was very busy for me. But Lizzy was now at playschool for two mornings. This gave me some thinking space to take in Aunty Ruby's letter and record my thoughts in my journal.

I listened to a song about the depth of trust we might know as we mature in our relationship with God – the simple trust of a child. For me it was a reassurance that God was taking me back to my childhood, holding my hand. It was only from a place of maturity that I would reclaim my childhood and recapture precious memories. He was helping me to invite him into it all and receive his healing love.

I still had no memory of Mum at the end. Those last six weeks we had together – September and October had been completely erased. Had the normality itself robbed me of memories? Or had they been blocked by my denial of grief? Yet more unanswered questions!

We invited Richard and Miriam over to see Aunty Ruby's letter. It was good to talk and share the memories it had stirred up. At my father's death we'd found some of his old diaries. Richard had one from 1961and I linked the dates and my father's comments with the information Aunty Ruby had given. Dad had referred to Mum as K.

April

> Weds 5th K was told that cancer was malignant
> Fri 7th Ruby came
> Sat 15th Ruby took Barbara back with her
> Weds 19th K to hospital
> Fri 21st K 1st operation

May

> Thurs 4th K 2nd operation
> Weds 17th K pleurisy
> Fri 26th K home – a joyful day indeed!

June

> Weds 14th Took K to Epsom hospital
> Tues 20th Barbara's birthday spent in Somerset
> Fri 30th Went to Somerset to collect Barbara

July

1st Returned with Barbara

22nd K picking up slowly but surely

Aug

Sat 19th Holiday in Jersey

Mon 28th All in sea – a lovely day

Thur 31st A lovely day – all bathing

Sept

2nd One of our best days

Returned home at night

Notes – This holiday was voted one of our best and the weather was good the second week. K bathed most days.

Oct

Fri 13th A black day

Sat 28th Ruby came

Tues 31st K to hospital

Nov

Thurs 2nd K 1st injection of Thistepa

Sat 4th 2nd injection

Sun 5th Ruby returned

Mon 6th Housekeeper employed

3rd injection

Wed 8th 4th injection

Fri 10th 5th injection

Notes The injections made K ill the following day. The drug killed the white corpuscles

Sun 12th 6th injection

Mon 13th K very ill and unable to keep food or drink down

Tue 14th 7th Injection postponed as blood count dangerously low

*Wed 15th Injection course abandoned as blood
count too low
Mon 20th K not responding to treatment as staff
had expected
Tue 21st Blood count not improving
Thur 23rd Only one visitor allowed (with mask and
gown) K isolated in separate room
Wed 29th No improvement in blood count – risk of
infection always present*

Dec

*Sat 2nd Took children to see K (Lexicon)
Sun 3rd K temperature 100
Mon 4th K worse – temperature 102 – no food
and vomiting all day – injection. Very very ill –
phoned Ruby
Tue 5th Phoned hospital 9.30 K no better
Phoned 11.30 K weaker
Arrived at hospital 12.30
Ruby arrived 8.00pm
Both at hospital all night
Wed 6th With K on and off up to 12.00 noon and
again from 5.15-5.45. Left Ruby with her
K passed away 7.45 pm
Thur 7th With Ruby to Undertakers and to hospital
and cemetery
Mon 11th Funeral 2.00 – 2.30. Home 3.10*

The letters and the diary entries together gave me the facts for
which I'd been searching. But they indicated several points
where my mum, my dad and Aunty Ruby had all been given
clues that time was running out. Why had nothing been said to
us? How could they have failed to realise that we also needed
this preparation?

We concluded that they were shielding us from a truth they
couldn't bear to face. They always hoped it wouldn't really come

to this. Mum might have got well and they would have upset us for nothing.

Also attitudes to children were far less inclusive than today. In the same way that children were restricted in hospital visiting, children were not given much medical information and not expected to ask for it. Our society has a history of 'protecting' children and pushing them aside. Our parents and Aunty Ruby were a product of that history before such ideas were questioned. In addition cancer wasn't spoken about and dying of it carried a stigma.

Nothing could change the past. But we determined that we would always be open with our children about illness. If we knew that death was a possibility we would tell them, even while believing for a miracle – a bit like taking out an insurance policy that one never really expects to need.

Another puzzling fact was the response of my grandmother. This was my mother's mother. How could she have been persuaded not to be at her daughter's funeral? If she had been there Aunty Ruby would have felt less pressured to rush away to see how she was coping.

Why wasn't she at the hospital? Why had she never come to visit her daughter in the nine months since we'd seen her that Easter? Was it her own ill health that had prevented her? She too was shocked by the news. Had no one told her that her daughter was dying? Was she being over-protected too?

I could hang on to bitterness about all this for the rest of my life. But what good would it do? It was yet another time to choose to forgive.

I'd forgotten the debilitating exhaustion that comes with grief. In this case my expression of grief was delayed. But I still couldn't escape the weariness of such emotional wear and tear and my journal records it.

Wednesday 18th January

> 'Feeling so tired. Life seems so busy and all I want
> to do is sleep or rest...

*...Help me get the kitchen more orderly. It gets
me down when it seems so chaotic and I don't
seem to have the energy to sort it out. Give me the
energy for your priorities for me today.*

*I'd like to write a long meaningful letter to Aunty
Ruby for her to receive with her birthday card,
which I'll need to post tomorrow. Help me write
something special and appreciative – expressing
what I want it to.'*

Her letter I knew had been costly – it would have brought back a lot of pain. And to have produced it at nearly 82 was remarkable. It would have taken her several attempts to write so much. I managed to write something in response, sharing some special memories and appreciating her role all through my life and that here she was again filling in the holes from the past.

Her response, though much shorter this time, was another letter I have treasured.

Dear Barbara,

*Thank you for the letter and card which arrived on
Monday. Thank you also for the lovely plant.*

*Your letter brought back some very nice
memories and reminded me of a few things I had
nearly forgotten. I shall read it several times yet
before I take it all in.*

*The tragedy of your mother's death gave us the
chance to get to know each other in a special way.
That has always stayed with me and always will.
My love for you and your love for me has always
been a very important thing in my life.*

*With love from
Aunty Ruby*

Life soon moved on again. But it had been a precious interlude to stop ... to look back and to take bigger steps on my journey back to my childhood. There were still occasions when I felt embarrassed to be dredging up the past. Was this a pity trip?

I took refuge in the fact that the friends I confided in were supportive. I was touched when Jill, her own grief still fresh, brought me flowers to acknowledge *my* grief. Indeed it validated my appraisal that it was time to release the sorrow that had been locked away so long.

Yes it had been a season to deal with some of the unfinished business. I had gathered information, grieved more fully and begun to forgive. The sieve had found the muck hidden deep within the well. It had brought it to light and was starting to eliminate it.

What helped me in the grief for my mum after Matthew's death?

- Yielding the grief to God
- Picture of the well – muck at the bottom that needed sieving out
- Acknowledgement that I hadn't said goodbye to my mum
- Asking the questions about her illness and death that I hadn't asked at the time or when I was growing up
- Keeping a journal to record my questions and express my feelings
- Richard's and Aunty Ruby's letters and my dad's diary and conversations in response
- Knowing the details of how my mum had died ('It's lovely!') and so feeling included in the death scene
- Being more in touch with my feelings and being able to express them
- Gratitude to God for preparing me as a child in memorising Psalm 23 and in giving me Aunty Ruby

- Having breast screening myself – facing up to what had happened
- Forgiving those who had failed to prepare me for her death
- Forgiving my grandmother for not coming to the funeral and then needing my aunt to go to her straight after the funeral
- Support of friends – acknowledging my grief and bringing flowers

What didn't help?

◊ Feeling embarrassed that I was dredging up the past

◊ Questioning whether I was looking for sympathy

7 *Ruby*

Ruby had been a significant person in my life. It was a real adventure to go to Aunty Ruby's for that eleven–week stay of my mum's final summer. She gave me a wonderful time. I still remember the strawberries from the garden, the cream teas and the trips to the park to the swings and slides. She and her friend, Joan, taught me new card games like Racing Demon. I had my 8th birthday with them and she gave me a wigwam.

She had always been kind and much loved. But that special time had forged a bond. It had been the opportunity to get to know each other well.

After my mum's death Ruby had become a mother figure, albeit at a distance. She bought my clothes in my childhood and looked out for my welfare. She visited each holiday. When I got married she had been a generous provider, enabling us to put down a deposit on our first home.

In terms of my grief journey, too, she had had a major role. She had been the one to tell me of my mum's death as a child. She had been the one to fill me in on the details over thirty years later.

Seven years after receiving that long letter about my mum's illness and death, I read a book by Teresa Seputis entitled, 'How to hear the voice of God in a noisy world'. It had questions to encourage listening to God. The idea was that you asked God questions and wrote down what you felt him saying. One day in August 01 the question was,

'Think back to the experience that most deeply hurt you. Ask God to speak about it. Ask how he can work his glory into it. Ask if there are areas where you need to forgive or be healed of pain.'

I considered the most painful experiences of my life – the death of my mum, my father's manic depression, relationship break-ups, the death of baby Michael, the miscarriage and the death of my father and then my unexpectedly agonised response to the death of Matthew. Which was most painful?

It's not easy to compare grief experiences objectively. But I found my thoughts returning to the death of my mum. Was there still unfinished business there? I knew that following Matthew's death I had processed a lot more of the grief. But now it seemed my attention was being drawn to the shock of her death. I had been so unprepared. My father and aunt couldn't realise that I was unable to read the signs they read. I felt again God urging me to forgive and release them from any expectation that they should have prepared me.

I had to take a step back here. I wasn't consciously holding anything against them. I knew they were just doing the best they knew. The thought that I needed to forgive them further came as a surprise. But I sensed it was true. Deep down I had felt robbed of preparation and kept in the dark.

So I prayed a prayer of forgiveness and release over both my father and my aunt. I had recently read a book about forgiveness ('Forgive, Release and Be Free' by Joff Day) which suggested praying blessing over those who have wronged you. I remembered my dream in which my father was having a great party in heaven. It seemed like he was already fully blessed! I imagined he had everything he could possibly want. But I wondered if the praying blessing might be important for me in terms of resolving the past – a declaration that I wanted only the best for him. So I expressed my desire that he enjoy the fullness of heaven.

Then I turned my thoughts to Aunty Ruby. I began praying blessing over her. As I did so, I felt God say, 'She needs to be prepared for her own death.'

This conversation was taking a very unexpected turn. What did this mean? How could she be prepared? Yet the words carried a weight of significance and urgency that arrested me. They were simple enough. In fact there was a clarity that I was beginning to recognise as a hallmark of the way God spoke to me. But it would be a challenge. It seemed God was asking something of me that was both exciting and daunting.

Aunty Ruby was always kind, always wise, always generous, always undemanding; always interested in everything I did – even when she didn't fully understand. My relationship with God had been an important part of my life since being baptised when I was 17. She had come to watch when Dad, Richard and I were all baptised together. She was always ready to support us but we never quite knew where she stood in terms of knowing God for herself. I'd tried to share my faith but there was a private side of her into which I'd never ventured. I knew she'd had a church upbringing but she hadn't regularly gone to church all the time I'd known her.

Could God be asking me to talk to her more directly than I ever had before? We talked weekly on the phone but this surely needed a visit. I wanted to say thank you for all she'd done for me now while we could both communicate freely. It would be so much better than the one-sided conversation of my last visit to my father. Perhaps more importantly, I also needed to give her opportunity to be confident of where she was going when she died. I wanted us both to be absolutely certain that we would be together one day along with my mum.

It was a long journey with three trains and a bus ride each way and it would take me all day. I was teaching full-time at Esher Church School and, though it was the summer holiday, I was trying to catch up on some desperately needed sorting and tidying out of cupboards. For a moment I felt I didn't have time.

Then the ridiculousness of that thought struck me. What was one day in my life for a much-loved lady who had given me so much! How could tidying out cupboards compare with establishing order for a precious aunt's final days and giving her the assurance of her eternal destiny? How topsy-turvy could my thinking get?

But I was nervous about how she would receive me in talking about eternal matters. As a headmistress she was used to wielding authority and she could sometimes be scary. Would she resent my intrusion? Would she feel affronted? Would it spoil our relationship?

She was 88. She had sold her bungalow and was in a residential home because she recognised she was nearing the end of her days. Would she be too old to understand?

There was a lot at stake. I asked Richard and Miriam and my own family to pray. The night before setting out I woke from a slightly restless sleep. Instantly I felt God reassure me with the words, 'It's not too late.' To be honest I was more concerned that she might respond badly than that she might be too old. But I took the words as encouragement for my venture.

The journey went well. I carried some photos of the family that I had mounted and framed. On the way I also bought some sunflowers. They looked bold – not a bit like how I felt!

On arrival I explained I'd wanted to see her while we could both talk. I contrasted this with saying goodbye to my father when he had lost the power of speech. I wanted to say a proper thank you and goodbye and be sure we were both ready for the time when she would be gone, however far away that might be. She seemed to understand.

The thank you bit was easy. She had done so much. She had had me stay for weekends when I was at college in Salisbury. She had welcomed Malcolm when we got engaged and given generously over the years. She was always ready to listen and give wise advice and I was particularly indebted to her for filling me in on the events surrounding my mum's death.

The next bit was much harder. I explained how I'd been led to make the journey. I referred to her church involvement when she was growing up. She latched on to this enthusiastically. Was she trying to reassure me and herself that she had a place in heaven? A cup of tea was brought in for her, interrupting our conversation. It was tempting to accept that was a natural conclusion. Could it be that I just needed to bring up the subject? Wasn't I giving her opportunity to ask if she wanted to know more?

But deep down I knew we were skating around the real issues. Inwardly praying fervently, I restated the purpose of my visit. I explained I wanted her to be fully prepared for her death. I wanted her to be totally sure that she would be going to God when she died. I made clear that going to church and the good life she had lived would not give her that absolute certainty. Only a living relationship with God could give her that confidence. I reminded her of when she'd been with my mum at the time of death and my mum had said, 'It's lovely' as she had seen heaven. I wanted Ruby to have the same kind of experience.

I had one or two little books with me. I used the pictures in them to communicate more clearly. I explained that, however good our lives are, we fall short of God's standard. Jesus had to die on the cross to take away all our wrongdoing. It's only as we ask for God's forgiveness on the basis of Jesus' death that we're forgiven and clean. There was a prayer at the end of the book to make a response. I knew she needed to make a commitment for herself. I explained it as like a parachute. It's provided to save you but it won't do so unless you pull the zip cord. The response needed to be real from her heart – it needed to be *her* decision.

Ruby listened thoughtfully. She was very quiet. I was aware it was an enormous challenge at 88 to reconsider the meaning she'd given her life. And it would need much humility to respond. I prayed silently.

Finally she said, 'Yes – I want to pray the prayer.' She began repeating the words after me. Suddenly she stopped. She started to cry. Something was blocking her. Then she said, 'It's my mum. I made that decision in my teens but my mum said, 'No, you're not a Christian – there's always one in the family who isn't.'

How extraordinary! A believing mother had robbed her daughter of a relationship with God. In accepting her mother's words, Ruby had lost confidence in her identity as a child of God! It was baffling how her mother had arrived at this conclusion. Was it simply too good to be true that all four of her children were Christians? But for over 70 years Ruby had been cheated by those words.

I talked about forgiveness, sharing with her what I'd learnt from 'Forgive, Release and Be Free'. I knew it was important to be specific about what she'd lost. Could she really forgive? She wasn't sure. She'd been robbed of a lot. There was a natural human resistance to forgive the one who had had such an enormous impact on her whole life. It was perfectly understandable. But it was getting in the way of Ruby recommitting her life to God and knowing that assurance that she could die in peace.

Had I come all this way for nothing after all? Had our conversation taken us so close only for this? What was I to do? I knew I was unlikely to have such an opportunity again. I looked to God for help. Into my mind flashed the words, 'It's not too late.' I told Ruby how I believed I'd heard these words from God in the night. She laughed and said, 'But it nearly is, isn't it?' With that she continued the prayer, committing her life to God.

I sent her a large print Bible and a magnifying sheet because her eyesight had deteriorated so much. But I was conscious she lived so far away and was unable to get to church. I wanted to connect her with people who could encourage her in her fresh response to God.

One morning this was particularly on my mind when I went to my local Baptist church. I asked the minister at the end of the service if he had any connections with churches in her area. He said he didn't but that he'd just spotted someone in the congregation who used to live in that area. I approached her with the same request.

Amazingly she was to have been in Leeds that Sunday but her plans had changed. She gave me the names of an elderly couple who lived very close. I rang them, explaining the situation. They sounded very caring and agreed to call on her. How amazing that God connected Ruby with people she could relate to so easily!

They visited her fortnightly. They prayed with her and obtained Bible reading notes in large print. They were a great support to her and she quickly described them as 'my friends'. She enthusiastically read the whole of the New Testament in a few months.

Ruby had her first stroke early one morning in February, eighteen months later when she was 90. John and Margaret (my cousins) found the Bible by her bed. Inside were dated Bible notes. They were folded open at the date of the day before.

I visited soon after her first stroke. I read Psalm 139.

O Lord, you have searched me
and you know me.
²You know when I sit and when I rise;
you perceive my thoughts from afar.
³You discern my going out and my lying down;
you are familiar with all my ways.
⁴Before a word is on my tongue
you know it completely, O Lord.

Verses 2 and 4 seemed particularly appropriate. She'd lost her speech. I could see how frustrated she was, not being able to say what she wanted. It was good that God knew everything on her mind and knew what she wanted to say. The hospital reassured me that she would regain her speech. She never did.

Ruby was in hospital for some time. When it was time for her to move back to the residential home, her room was no longer available. She was given a much smaller room. Soon it became apparent that she would need more nursing than this home could offer.

My cousins lived in Somerset too. My cousin, Margaret, found another home and I visited it with her that April. We thought Ruby would be happy there. She was soon settled in a large double-aspect room with a lovely view.

Her inability to speak was a great loss. So often she'd wanted me to share with her the events of my life and for many years our main contact had been by phone. The distance between us now seemed to separate us so much more. I often rang the home to enquire after her but it wasn't the same as the weekly phone calls with Ruby that we'd enjoyed for many years. Visits were so much more important now. I was teaching full-time but I visited each holiday.

It was October of the following year when Margaret rang to say Ruby wasn't as well. She'd had a number of strokes and chest infections and they had weakened her and she didn't seem as focused and interested in life.

Fortunately it was half term week. I quickly rearranged my plans so I could visit. I caught the three trains to Taunton and rang for a taxi. I asked him to stop at a florist's for me to buy some flowers. I bought some pink and white lilies.

Ruby was in bed. It was the first time she'd been in bed since my visits to her in hospital. Today she hadn't wanted to get up, though she looked better than I'd expected. She was sleepy but she grasped my hand. I explained that I'd heard she wasn't so well and I wanted to say goodbye. I said I realised she might live for another 5 years but I wanted to be sure not to miss saying goodbye. She understood.

I thanked her again for all she'd done in my life. She smiled as I reminded her of my memories – particularly of the time three years before when she'd recommitted her life to God. I was so glad we'd said a 'goodbye' then while we could both speak. I reassured her we would meet again in heaven.

I read Psalm 23 and Psalm 139. Then I prayed in line with these. I remembered how I'd read Psalm 139 after her stroke. This time it was verses 13 to 16 that struck me – particularly verse 16.

¹³For you created my inmost being;
you knit me together in my mother's womb.
¹⁴I praise you because I am fearfully and wonderfully made;
your works are wonderful,
I know that full well.
¹⁵My frame was not hidden from you
when I was made in the secret place.
When I was woven together in the depths of the earth,
¹⁶your eyes saw my unformed body.
All the days ordained for me
were written in your book
before one of them came to be.

God knew how many pages were left in her book – I felt there were only a few.

I talked of heaven and she enjoyed the pictures I created for her. I encouraged her that it was more beautiful than anything we'd seen on earth and she smiled. She was always interested in hearing about my life so I told her about my new classroom and my class. But today she was far away. She was much more interested in heaven. I talked about the view from her window but it was like she wasn't seeing it. I felt she was more attuned to heaven than earth.

The lilies were put on her window-sill. I was glad I was giving them while she was alive so she could see them her last few days and be reminded of my visit. It struck me that I could be buying flowers after her death and that I preferred her to enjoy them while she could appreciate them.

I felt to take spiritual authority over any pain. I don't know if she was concerned by my slightly raised voice but she sat up very straight – maybe concerned for me. I prayed peace over her and released her to God's timing.

As I left she waved goodbye – very clearly. It was the last time I saw her.

Ten days later I woke at 4.50. I'd been warned again by the home that she was near the end. My thoughts turned to her immediately. I consciously placed her again into God's hands. I rang the Home at 5.20. and was told she'd died just after 5.00. I felt privileged that God had wakened me so I could share in her departure, though separated by so many miles. An hour later a song inspired by Psalm 116 was on my mind, commanding my attention. I read the psalm.

'I love the Lord, for he heard my voice;
he heard my cry for mercy.
8For you, O Lord, have delivered my soul from death, my eyes
*   from tears,*
my feet from stumbling,
9that I may walk before the Lord
in the land of the living.
15Precious in the sight of the Lord
is the death of his saints. Praise the Lord.

Just like the psalm I'd read, I knew God had received Ruby as a precious gift. Like her name, Ruby, she was truly precious as a precious stone both to us and to God. I marvelled that she was now walking before the Lord with a new body – able to talk, able to sing, able to eat, able to run and jump and dance.

Grateful that I'd had this special uninterrupted time away from the busyness of the day, I quickly got myself ready to go to school to teach. I was so thankful for all the preparation for her death, especially the time three years before, when she'd recommitted her life to God. I was glad too for my visit ten days before and that sense that very morning that it was a significant time for her.

On arriving at school I was suddenly aware of the enormity of this event in my life. Her death had been so anticipated that I'd somehow failed to appreciate the impact it would have. Teaching is so all-absorbing that it tends to obliterate all other concerns. Four and five year olds are particularly demanding. But by lunch-time I realised being in school wasn't having its usual anaesthetic effect. My mind was elsewhere. I had to have some space. I needed time away from school to absorb the fact of her death and to grieve.

I sought permission for time off. I was reassured that I would be allowed a day off for the funeral but it was obviously tricky to grant me time right now to grieve. And yet I knew I would be unable to give myself to the children in my present state. Would they really be safe with me? I felt distant and not confident that I would respond appropriately to them. Perhaps no one else knew exactly how I felt. I would just need to be assertive, I decided. After all it was a bit like being ill – only you yourself know what you can and can't manage. I asked for cover for the next day before leaving.

It struck me as ironic that my instinctive response had been to dash off to school as normal. It was exactly the same as when my mum had died. Then I was the pupil – now I was the teacher. Then I'd been whisked straight to school soon after hearing the news. This time it had been my 'choice', though I hadn't actually stepped back sufficiently to consider any alternative – I was just functioning in automatic mode. But at least now it was dawning on me that I did need time to absorb the information. It was a little belated but I was learning.

I returned home wrung out like a rag doll. It had been an early start and I needed space to be refreshed and time with God. I went to bed – a favourite place to read and meditate and pray. Into my mind came a picture of a silver chalice like one that might be used for communion. Pondering this I reread Psalm 116 that I had read early that morning and noted verse 13

'I will lift up the cup of salvation
and call on the name of the Lord.'

It was a clear reminder to me to focus on Ruby's salvation. I thought of the words often quoted in a communion service,

'In the same way, after supper he took the cup, saying, "This cup
is the new covenant in my blood; do this, whenever you drink it,
in remembrance of me." For whenever you eat this bread and
drink this cup, you proclaim the Lord's death until he comes.'

(1 Cor. 11:25-26)

I spent the next day at home. It was a valuable day. I lay on my bed and recorded my thoughts and emotions. It helped me process them.

I decided to study the use of 'cup' in the Bible. I discovered that as well as salvation it referred to suffering as when Jesus begs 'May this cup be taken from me. I marvelled at the truth that it was because Jesus drank the cup of suffering and grief that we can drink the cup of salvation. I wrote out a prayer declaration, incorporating these thoughts.

'I commit today to God. I trust him to help me use it as he wants – to help me grieve in the way he wants. My Father is looking after me. I receive his love.

I call on Jesus to be my salvation. He has delivered me in the past from the chains of guilt and shame (from inability to express my grief), from abandonment and vulnerability, from accusation and from grief itself. The blood of Jesus has bought my freedom. His death destroyed him who holds the power of death. Jesus tasted death for me. He has taken the sting from death. Death has been swallowed up in victory.'

As I prayed I became increasingly aware that my aunt's death was triggering so many associations with my mum. After all they were sisters. Also my aunt had been a mum to me in so many ways. I sensed something was prolonging my grief, connecting them both to me unhelpfully. Could it be that there were ties that now needed to be severed? I felt a little out of my depth in dealing with them alone. I went to a friend for prayer.

She severed in prayer unhelpful connections with my aunt and then my mum. I saw in my mind an image of myself holding my mum's hand and wanting to carry her into the rest of my life. I made a conscious decision to let go. As I released her hand, Jesus offered me his hand instead. We walked along the path together. Where there were obstacles, he led the way, finding the best route.

My friend encouraged me to take the time I needed to grieve – to take time off work and to cancel arrangements. I was meant to be speaking at the school prayer group. When I've committed myself to something I don't like to cancel and let anyone down. But slowly I was coming to the conclusion that there were times when it was appropriate. Perhaps it was all part of acknowledging my needs and respecting them – something I had never found easy. Anyway I rang and found my speaking engagement was easily moved. I cancelled one or two other arrangements and found people supportive and understanding.

I was fine to go back to school the next day. Of course there was still a grieving process to work through, but I knew something significant had happened. I had let go. A couple of days later, another friend said she had a picture in her mind of Jesus holding my hand. It was a lovely reminder of the image I had seen myself – a confirmation that he would take care of me and lead the way.

The following week was the funeral. I had the immense privilege of giving the address. I told the story of this chapter. I remembered too the dream I'd had when my father died and I was also struck by her name as being a precious stone and the words I'd read so soon after her death, 'Precious in the sight of the Lord is the death of his saints.' I incorporated these thoughts into my closing words.

'So today though we miss her and grieve for our loss, it's a day of celebration – joy and excitement and anticipation. The best is yet to come. Imagine the best party. Food is being passed around – fantastic party food. Music is accompanying an amazing firework display. Petals in pastel colours are raining down, floating gently and falling on everyone like confetti. Today Aunty Ruby is being welcomed and honoured. As we say goodbye, heaven says, 'Welcome. Let's celebrate. We delight in this precious jewel.'

Malcolm had driven the three hour journey each way. But next day I was the exhausted one. It was hard to drag myself off to school again but it was difficult to ask for any more time. It was another reminder that emotion is fatiguing.

I kept a pink lily from the flowers on her coffin. I placed it on my windowsill. It reminded me of the lilies I'd taken her on my final visit. I was so glad she'd had them to enjoy in her final few days. And I relished the memory of that visit and her focus on heaven. Now she was enjoying the fullness of it.

What helped?

- Saying a proper goodbye three years before
- Knowing she was prepared for death i.e. we both knew where she was going
- The Home indicating her death was imminent
- Seeing her shortly before her death and having opportunity to say goodbye then
- Her goodbye wave in recognition that it was final

- Waking early that morning and sensing I was being prepared
- Understanding better that, although I had intellectually acknowledged that I was ready for her death, I still needed space to grieve
- Knowing better how I respond to grief and what I needed
- Support and understanding of those affected by my cancelling of arrangements
- Freedom to speak at the funeral and share my memories etc.
- Awareness that her death linked in with unfinished business with Mum
- Prayer to break ties with her and with my mum

What didn't help?

- ◊ Going to school to teach as if life could carry on as normal
- ◊ Difficulty in getting time off
- ◊ Returning to school the day after the funeral, totally exhausted

What could help?

- Feeling embarrassed that I was dredging up the past
- Questioning whether I was looking for sympathy

8 *Still More about Mum*

Was I finally learning to say goodbye? In Ruby's death I'd been able to outwork much that I'd learnt about preparing for death and about grieving. Somehow, too, the fact that she was my mum's sister had given me opportunity to revisit my mum's death and bring more closure.

In fact it triggered the opportunity to receive more prayer from a couple of friends. On the evening we met at my home to pray, one had listened to her car radio on the way over and had heard that a radio play was to be broadcast that evening – 'The Resurrection of Miss Pym' – in fact Barbara Pym. How extraordinary!

I knew that Barbara Pym, the novelist, shared my name, only the extra 'm' in my surname distinguishing us. But it seemed so significant that a play with such a title was to be broadcast that evening. Was God fostering trust that a 'new me' was about to come to life?

That night we explored issues of self-blame, condemnation and shame and self-rejection. I saw a black poison inside me from which I was recoiling. But then Jesus flushed it away, leaving me light, clear and clean.

So often I'd felt I wasn't a proper person and felt inferior and incompetent. But God was reassuring me that he loved me and accepted me just as I was. It was indeed a resurrection evening.

God was showering me with jewels like a princess. One of my friends shared these verses with me:

'O afflicted city, lashed by storms and not comforted,

I will build you with stones of turquoise,
your foundations with sapphires.
¹²I will make your battlements of rubies,
your gates of sparkling jewels,
and all your walls of precious stones.'

(Isaiah 54:11-12)

Appropriately, the ministry tool we were using was called 'Restoring the Foundations'. God was restructuring my life, painstakingly building something of immense value. And, could it be that what I had learnt through Ruby's death was contributing to the 'battlements of rubies'?

Surely my healing was now complete and it was time to work on this book. I felt I now had a little understanding of what had helped in my grieving process and what was less helpful. I wanted to share what I'd learnt, hopeful that it might benefit others who were grieving.

I'd also been attending a preaching class for beginners. Might I one day have opportunity to speak at weekend conferences on grief? I wanted to hone my public speaking skills ready.

The tutor observed that I needed to work on my voice – it was too gentle and quiet. A neighbour and friend, Anne, gladly agreed to give me voice lessons. She suggested voice exercises and listened to my sermons. One Friday evening at my lesson, I was having difficulty. I observed that my natural tendency was to let my voice die away and I was battling to deliver phrases with the passion they deserved.

'Why am I struggling so much with this?' I asked Anne.

She paused for a moment. 'I think it's to do with difficulty expressing emotion,' she responded. 'It means there's less colour in your voice.'

Instantly I knew she'd touched on something. But could there really still be more? Yet there was a confirming acknowledgement deep within that her words were true.

I was still pondering on this, two days later. I happened to be attending a writer's conference. One of the speakers had offered individual appointments for would-be authors with a sample of their work. I took along an extract from an earlier version of my chapter on Michael. She encouraged me on style and use of language but said 'It lacks emotion.'

I was baffled. Two comments within two days seemed to authenticate the need to delve deeper. But how? Who could help me?

The next day, driving back from school, my thoughts returned to these questions. How could I deal with these issues? How could I put colour in my voice and in my writing?

The route home was a journey I took every weekday. But there was an unusual queue of traffic at a roundabout that in my preoccupied state of mind I'd failed to anticipate. Suddenly I found it difficult to change lane to take my usual route. Bizarrely I was being forced to take the A3.

Feeling puzzled and rather foolish that after eight years I was deviating almost involuntarily from my normal route, I was suddenly stunned by the view before me. For arched across the A3 was the most wonderful double rainbow. I love rainbows. Musing gratefully that I could so easily have missed this, I noted that the colours were much more vibrant than usual.

Thanking God for the rainbow I queried, 'Is there some significance in this? Was it you redirecting my route so I could see it? Why are the colours so vivid?'

Then flashed into my mind the questions I'd been asking a few minutes before. 'How could I put colour in my voice and in my writing?' It was clear that God was reassuring me. He was the author of colour. He who put the colours in the rainbow could as easily put back into my life the expression of colour in emotion. And that first rainbow in the Bible, after Noah's Ark came to rest, was a promise from God of his protection. God was affirming his care for me.

As to the route… I'd no idea how to go about this. But if God could redirect me when I was driving a route 'in automatic mode', surely he could direct me in the unseen realm and lead me along the route where I would discover the colour.

It was an amazing experience... so personal. I was in awe that God had placed that rainbow there for me. Yet, as always, there is soon the temptation to discount it and regard it as fanciful. Was I simply trying to justify my stupidity in taking such an indirect route home?

I had a prearranged gathering with friends that evening. We would pray silently, listening to God. I didn't share my experience or refer to it in any way. But, incredibly, one lady said that, in the time of quiet, she'd seen a picture of a rainbow. I could hardly believe my ears when she stated categorically it was to do with healing of the emotions.

It was a couple of months later that I saw a flyer advertising a Cruse meeting. I found I could undergo training to become a Cruse counsellor. A new course was starting early the following year.

On the course we watched a video on children's grief. The objectivity of the training context gave me a fresh perspective. Instead of blaming myself for not grieving properly over my mum's death, I started to see where things had been handled unhelpfully. I hadn't been given space to grieve. I hadn't been encouraged to express any emotion. With a scary teacher at school and my home instantly changed by having a resident housekeeper, there had been no safe places. At last I could acknowledge that things could have been handled differently.

The course providers had reassured us that it was common for training to trigger emotions. So I spoke to a wise experienced lady in the break. She listened compassionately to my story and recommended I consider writing to my mum and finding my own way to say goodbye.

So I poured out my heart in a letter to my mum. I told her how I'd longed for a goodbye... that I'd have loved to see her in hospital ... to exchange letters ...to have been included along with the adults.

I saw for the first time my need to forgive *her* not just for dying but for the lack of a goodbye. And I caught a glimpse of the agony of heart she'd endured in leaving us. The exclusion, however misguided, was intended only to protect me – to shield me from a reality she could barely face herself.

Previously I'd beaten myself up over the lack of a goodbye. Maligning myself had become habitual. My 'resurrection' evening had shown me how wrong that was. But on a daily basis it was so hard to change. A complete stranger mimed a picture he felt God had shown him for me. I was to take off my boxing gloves and stop attacking myself and instead lift my hands to God in worship.

I asked God more about this. How did it relate to my journey through grief? I had a sense that my early grief had opened a wound within me where I turned on myself. I blamed myself for existing – for causing trouble to my family, the neighbours, the housekeepers. I blamed myself for not grieving in the 'right' way – for not crying or talking about my mum, for not being able to express emotion. I blamed myself for being different from other children.

I had an illuminating dream. In this dream I opened the Bible and was trying to read Psalm 103. But in the binding and obstructing my vision were black and white photos of myself as a child. On waking I read the psalm. It began,

'Praise the Lord ...
³who forgives all your sins
and heals all your diseases,
⁴who redeems your life from the pit ...'

This dream confirmed for me that issues from my childhood were blocking my full healing and release from the pit. But it pointed to a God who through forgiveness and restoration would come to my rescue. The black and white of the photos, authentic in that my early photos *were* all black and white, seemed starkly anachronistic – inappropriate relics from the past. And again there was that imagery of lack of colour. Aspects of my childhood were indeed bleakly grey and sombre. But I was now looking to God not only for colour in my life but also for the articulation of the full spectrum of emotion.

The psalm underlined God's compassion, gentleness and forgiveness.

⁸The Lord is compassionate ...
⁹He will not always accuse, ...
¹²as far as the east is from the west,
so far has he removed our transgressions from us.'

Clearly I had much to learn from that in relation to myself. It was time to stop accusing myself. If God himself was forgiving, gentle and compassionate towards me, I needed to reflect his heart and be forgiving, gentle and compassionate towards myself. And running through the whole was the exhortation to praise God – just as the giver of the boxing glove picture had urged me.

So how could I appropriate this psalm? How could I deal with these issues blocking my full healing? Obviously there was still more to be done.

I discovered Ellel – a Christian healing centre with a mission to proclaim the Kingdom of God by preaching the good news, healing the broken-hearted and setting the captives free. I went to a personal healing retreat there. I had two prayer ministers who gently explored my past. I had never consciously resented those who had unwittingly made it hard for me to say goodbye. But somehow speaking aloud my forgiveness in prayer enabled me to see that my self-hatred was misplaced. I needed only to forgive myself for hating myself! The truth was beginning to release me layer by layer.

I was told that inhibiting the expression of emotion was an ungodly self-control. The result was often to internalise emotion, leading to depression. They prayed for the full release of grief. I think we were all expecting me to cry. But nothing obvious happened.

So the session came to a close and I went to the bookshop. I lingered there a few minutes sheltering from the heavy rain I could hear outside. I mused that the heavens were shedding the tears I couldn't let flow. When the downpour had subsided a little, I emerged to make my way to the dining hall for tea. Amazingly there was a beautiful rainbow across my path.

Surely it was a sign! I was touched by God's reassurance. Whether I cried or not was insignificant. I just needed to trust that

God was at work and bringing healing. He would release that full spectrum of emotion.

So God had done his bit. How could I cooperate? What was my role?

I knew I had to change in the way I regarded myself and believe what the Bible declared about me. The freedom in Christ teaching and books by Neil Anderson helped reinforce this. But somehow on a daily basis, such truths seemed to elude me, remaining theoretical and remote.

I was particularly keen to address the habitual self-destructive insults I was used to hurling at myself. Could it be that the compulsion to keep working was rooted in the same desire to punish myself? I wanted too to address the anxiety and people-pleasing which might be traced to insecurity from my childhood.

I wrote a prayer to help me accomplish this. I declared it day after day for months. It invited God to bridge my biblical understanding with the ways I responded in everyday life.

It included,

> '*Thank you for loving and accepting me just as I am. I receive your love. Teach me to love myself as you do and to be patient, kind and forgiving of myself. Holy Spirit, please alert me when I don't speak well of myself or treat myself unkindly. I choose to speak words of life and encouragement to myself and give myself time to relax and enjoy life. When I feel unworthy or ashamed or trapped by my past, I remember I'm a new creation – the old has gone – the new has come. Everything in my life is new – a gift from you.*
>
> *... When I feel stressed I choose not to feel sorry for myself. I forgive anyone who is making my life more difficult and I bless them in your name. You mature me through difficulties. Show me your perspectives. I choose to act on what you show me and please you rather than other people. I submit*

> *my expectations of myself and others' expectations*
> *of me to you, my Father.*
> *I yield my body, soul and spirit to be totally*
> *yours today for your glory. Tear down the mental*
> *strongholds that prevent me from seeing what you*
> *want to do. I yield to the Holy Spirit to walk in the*
> *fullness of your purposes for my life. I declare that*
> *you will give Malcolm and me all we need to fulfil*
> *your perfect plans for us. I commit our way to you.*
> *I lay at your feet everything that concerns me. I*
> *trust you. You will work things out because you are*
> *faithful. Use everything to teach me to depend on*
> *you. You are watching over my life and leading me*
> *in your paths.'*

I discovered that these positive declarations were so much more helpful than a beseeching-type prayer. These statements of faith injected hope and confidence in God into my whole being. And I noticed that bit by bit I *was* becoming more positive and less inclined to run myself down.

I discovered St Ignatius' examen. This is a form of reflection in which you look back over the day. One aspect is to identify the thing for which you're most grateful and the thing for which you're least grateful. This alerted me to emotions which might have lain buried and unacknowledged. Recording these in a journal helped me explore more deeply how I really felt – the positive emotions – joy, pleasure and excitement and the negative – pain, irritation, frustration, guilt and despair.

Another tool for identifying my feelings and expressing them was movement. I noted that, in the Bible, mourning and wailing were contrasted with dancing.

> *'a time to weep and a time to laugh,*
> *a time to mourn and a time to dance,'*

> *'You turned my wailing into dancing;*

you removed my sackcloth and clothed me with joy,
¹²that my heart may sing to you and not be silent.
O Lord my God, I will give you thanks for ever.'

(Eccles. 3:4 and Psalm 30:11-12)

I love words. But there was something so expressive and immediate about movement – it seemed a purer form of communication. Could it be more closely aligned with right brain activity and thought at its very simplest?

As one who found it difficult to express herself in any form, it took perseverance to become less inhibited. Yet it seemed an appropriate way to counter the emotional suppression which had been habitual from my childhood. I had a sense that God was freeing me at the very core of my being.

Often I was overly concerned with how I looked and what people thought of me. Indeed much of my movement was private – just me with God and occasionally with a close friend too. However, the times I did manage to step out of my comfort zone took me into greater freedom. There was a releasing of both my spirit and my soul, and a yielding to God which made me bolder in other areas of my life.

My Cruse training was now completed. I was impressed by what I saw and I began working as a Cruse volunteer myself. My clients' stories were sad – their expressions of pain familiar, though always different – always harrowing. I found it challenging, yet rewarding, heart-wrenching yet a joy.

The following year I undertook training with Cruse to help children too. This gave me the opportunity to reflect on the amazing transformation I'd experienced in my own life. One aspect of this was creating the picture I referred to in the Introduction.

I was no longer imprisoned by grief as I'd been as a child. I'd walked through the open gate. I believed I could help those who were feeling confused and trapped, isolated and misunderstood.

I left teaching to free up more time for bereavement work. After a year of working with children with Cruse, I additionally took a part-time job working for another bereavement charity,

Jigsaw4u – now Jigsaw(SouthEast). This provides therapeutic group activities for bereaved children and their families.

The groups enable each person to share their grief experiences with their peers. This helps them feel less isolated. In addition, the fact that each family member partakes of the same activities (within their own age-group) creates opportunity to share memories and facilitates communication in the family.

So... the sharing of grief both with peers and within the family! Two aspects so much on my heart! Sometimes I catch a glimpse of that little girl I once was and see another trapped, lonely child. I watch with wonder as she finds words to express her grief and her memories, while participating in craft activities with other children and having fun too.

But for me the balloon release was especially moving. At the first group I attended I was free to participate myself. Bizarrely it happened to take place on my birthday – the anniversary of the day my mum had brought me into the world – the day the umbilical cord was cut! Now it was my turn to 'cut the cord' that had held me to her – a final releasing of that suppressed grief that had weighed me down so long. And for me to let go of that balloon addressed to my mum was paradoxically a precious birthday gift – I attached a luggage label on which I wrote,

> *'Now I know a little of how much it must have hurt you to leave us. See you one day.*
>
> *Lots of love B.'*

So much had changed in my life! That little girl who had felt cheated of a goodbye and had been trapped by her held-in grief was no more. I'm so grateful to God for his healing and his understanding, enabling me to connect with that child and take steps in learning to grieve.

Just as the prophecy had promised, God had enabled me to release that child to him for him to raise. As a child I'd been too old for my years. Now I have more joie de vivre ... am more fun-loving ... am more childishly excited than ever. Am I reclaiming the childhood I missed out on?

As a mum myself I glimpse something of the pain my mum must have suffered in leaving us. I'm so grateful that I've had the privilege of seeing my four children become adults of whom I am really proud. Despite my own lack of mothering, God has made me a mum like I wanted to be. Could that mothering extend beyond my own family? Could my life help others find freedom too as I share my steps in learning to grieve?

I watched that balloon rise into the clouds till it became the tiniest dot and then could be seen no more. This time I knew I had let go. It was a final goodbye.

What helped?

- Recognising more healing was needed

- Assurance that God had promised that the full spectrum of my emotions would be restored

- Being open to further prayer ministry from trusted sources

- Exploring grief issues through Cruse, especially looking objectively at how children need to say goodbye, need to have space to grieve and be encouraged to express emotion

- Inviting God's searchlight to show me any areas where I still needed healing

- Forgiving my mum for the lack of a goodbye

- Recognising I was blaming myself for not grieving in the 'right' way and for being different from other children

- Forgiving myself for my mistreatment of myself, asking God to alert me where this had become habitual

- Declaring in daily prayer God's acceptance of me and his good plans for my life.

- Reflecting each day on the events for which I was most grateful and least grateful and journaling these and my emotions to help me acknowledge my feelings

- Dance – using it to express myself

- Helping others in their bereavements – recognition that there were lessons I'd learned and even the mistakes I'd made had taught me what was helpful and what was less helpful – seeing myself as a victor rather than a victim

- Balloon release – letting go of the grief

Conclusion

Well, that's my story. I don't know how I would have been without those six deaths. But I do know they've shaped me. My life has been enriched by loss.

I hope my journey will enable you to take your own steps if you are grieving – to put you in touch with your own emotions and to find the best ways to say goodbye. Certain themes seemed to recur so I now propose to draw those together. These may also give some guidelines to help others who are grieving.

Facts

Being given factual information seems to be a key part of processing the reality of death. Hearing the details, however bizarre or outside of our experience, apparently helps us make sense of it. Having little information distances us unhelpfully and interferes with the processing.

This can sometimes be overlooked when young children are involved but communicating with them in an age-appropriate way will facilitate their grieving process. Jigsaw4u and Jigsaw(SouthEast) offer a Doctor's Spot for families attending their bereavement groups. This allows all to ask the questions they may have not felt free to ask before. Even children as young as five are given a simple medical explanation as to why the death occurred. Everyone who suffers loss of someone close needs to know what happened and the events surrounding the death. If this stage is missed out the child will need to return to it in later life to find full healing.

Where a death is anticipated it is helpful if this is spelt out to a child. Both the nature of the illness and the seriousness of it, need to be communicated clearly. The child will sense that something is going on and will be unsettled by the mystery and feel excluded. Eda LeShan states in her book *Learning to Say Good-by*, '... a child can live through *anything*, so long as he or she is told the truth and is allowed to share with loved ones the natural feelings people have when they are suffering.'

Just like we take out insurance for things we don't really believe will ever happen to us, it can be explained to the child that we really hope the death won't happen yet (and maybe not for years), but that the doctors have said it might, so we'll be thinking about it just in case.

Holding or viewing the body after death is a very individual decision. It's important to think seriously about this and be guided by your own feelings. Some people find the thought traumatic. Others find it helps them accept the reality of death and it gives them peace.

Space to grieve

Everyone needs time to take in the news of the death and to start to grieve. Sometimes we can be tempted to distract people, especially children, by keeping them busy or entertained. But children seem to have a natural ability to dip in and out of grief and will grieve in short bursts interspersed with play if allowed. It seems they have their own safety valves to prevent their grieving becoming too intense and harmful for them. Allowing them to share in the conversation of other family members and be involved in the funeral arrangements, if they want to, helps establish in their minds the reality and significance of the death.

We could learn from the Jewish tradition of seven days in which the bereaved stays home, away from school and work supported by relatives and friends who sit with him to share in the grief without the need for words. They understand that comforting those who mourn isn't the same as distracting them. Their goal isn't to get them to talk. Their presence is saying: "I'm here for you. I feel your pain. There are no words." Family, friends and neighbours take care of their needs, running errands and taking on any public commitments. This provides an atmosphere of care and love which helps bring healing.

Opportunity to say Goodbye

If the death is anticipated there may be opportunity before death to say goodbye. It's helpful if we can overcome our embarrassment and acknowledge that death may not be far away (while perhaps mitigating this with the statement that we may be mistaken and it may yet be years off). We can explain that we want to say goodbye before it becomes more difficult. This is a time to express gratitude and maybe ask for forgiveness relating to any unfinished business. It might be a time to make funeral plans or simply share special memories together.

Children are often not given the chance through overprotectiveness or the belief that they are too young to understand. But the exclusion may be felt as rejection. Children understand a lot more than we give them credit for. Hospitals are now much more aware of the impact on children but sometimes adults need encouragement to include them.

Similarly the funeral is another time to say goodbye. The child who is not allowed to attend may later feel pushed out. He may feel unvalued and insignificant as he puzzles over why he wasn't included in this special family time.

Sharing Feelings and Memories

In the same way that children may not be given space to grieve, they may not be encouraged to share their feelings and memories. Even adults are sometimes encouraged to take their minds off the bereavement and pick up social activities as a distraction whereas they need people to listen while they share. Sometimes we need to give ourselves and others permission to grieve.

It's helpful if the bereaved can be encouraged to cry and ask questions. Freedom to share feelings honestly, rather than feeling obliged to pretend everything is fine, will help them process their grief more healthily.

Children are particularly sensitive to adult emotion and will be reluctant to share if it appears to be upsetting a parent. Opportunities to meet with other children or young people their age, who are also experiencing loss, enables them to find ways to articulate their grief. Bereavement groups run by Jigsaw4u and Jigsaw(SouthEast) are helpful here. The creative activities these provide (e.g. memory boxes and salt jars) also offer therapeutic expression.

Writing down feelings whether in journal form or pictorially can be valuable. This might be an opportunity to record questions, insights and one's own responses to grief. Being absolutely honest with oneself can be very healing. Or we can address these thoughts to God either in spoken or written prayer. God is big enough to handle our barrage of emotion and in the process of reflection we may receive new insights and deeper peace, especially if we consciously yield the emotion to him and ask him for his perspective.

The bereaved person might choose, from a range of objects, one that symbolises how he is feeling. This can become a powerful metaphor – identifying emotion at a deeper level than normal speech and offering a form of communication in which to articulate one's grief. For young people and uninhibited older ones dance could be used in this way too.

Reading of the emotions of others can be a springboard to recognise one's own. This could be the Psalms or other poetry or the biographies of others who have experienced loss or pain. I hope this book might have a role here whether you connect with my emotions or whether it helps you identify emotions and thoughts of your own that makes you the unique and special person you are.

Receiving letters and cards that share particular memories is often extraordinarily precious and comforting. Friends with whom you can share your innermost feelings are invaluable. People often feel reticent because they don't know what to say. You can reassure them that 'just' listening is so important.

No words would ever be adequate anyway. In fact, people trying to provide answers can often be even more upsetting. Talking openly with other family members can also be healing, but it can be tricky to know whether one's reminiscences are welcomed or upsetting unless this has been discussed together.

Bereavement organisations have a valuable role here. I'm personally familiar with Jigsaw4u, Cruse and Winston's Wish and had very helpful training from Fegan's. See Appendix A for more information on these. The opportunity to speak with someone outside of one's own family situation enables one to speak freely without having to be sensitive to the feelings of other family members.

Each operates in a confidential way. Some offer support for individuals and others for the family as a whole. The grief support worker can listen impartially. Often he or she can reassure the bereaved person that what is being experienced is normal and it will not always be so acutely painful.

Receiving love and being grateful

Love is healing however expressed. It's good to allow people to give to you. Let them know you appreciate their flowers, their meals, their hugs and their prayers. Gratitude is healing and helps to counter the self-pity which is a natural part of loss but, if unchecked, can slow down the grieving process.

It's good to recognise that we can't change what has happened but we *can* choose our responses. Choosing to worship is an extension of this. But we also need to be real with God and express to him the emotions we are carrying. We can't miss out that stage. David, writer of many of the Psalms, seems to have grasped the need to blend absolute honesty with a heart of worship. Reading these can help us find that balance.

Forgiveness

This may not be required in every grief experience but sometimes it is necessary to forgive the person for dying. Often too at such a time people may misunderstand your response to grief or may act in a way that is hurtful when you are already feeling fragile. Being ready to forgive oils the relationships and releases us from the damaging effects self-pity engenders.

Feelings of guilt need to be expressed. Others can often see more clearly that we had the best intentions and can reassure us when we doubt ourselves. But then there needs to be a forgiving of ourselves and a receiving of God's forgiveness.

Letting go

Learning to hope again is perhaps the final stage of the grieving process. It is in no way a denial of your love for the one who has died but an acknowledgement that this is what they would want of you. So it is perhaps receiving their final gift to you.

It is indeed a recognition that your life has entered a new season with new hopes and new aspirations. Finding a symbolic way to express this can be helpful. It could be a balloon release or simply opening a door and stepping over the threshold to a new life beyond.

It's time to say goodbye!

Appendix A
Support and Resources for
Bereaved Children and Families

Bereavement is one of the most devastating losses that we experience and may bring profound changes to a young person's life. Losing a parent, sibling or grandparent may leave the young person feeling vulnerable and overwhelmed and fearful of losing another family member. Young people bereaved of a parent often feel different and isolated from their peers and perhaps retreat into withdrawal or suffer depression. It may be their first experience of death and raise issues of their own mortality and fears of the future.

The family may be able to support the grieving young person by listening and encouraging him to express his feelings. Parents may reassure him it's ok to be sad, angry and cry. Family members may offer opportunities to share memories and still find ways to have fun and laugh.

But often grieving families find it hard to know when is an appropriate time to talk and express feelings and share memories. In fact their very sensitivity to one another may lead to a reticence to discuss these things for fear of upsetting one another further. Young people are often particularly anxious not to upset a parent and may avoid all discussion.

Connecting with other families in the same situation

Jigsaw4u is based in Mitcham and works in the SW London area with children suffering from trauma. In partnership with the Taylor Foundation and Macmillan they provide support to children with a family member affected by life-threatening illness. Its sister charity, **Jigsaw(SouthEast)** supports bereaved families in Surrey, Sussex and Kent through Family Groups. They also provide support, in partnership with Macmillan, for children with a family member affected by life-threatening illness. Contacts for both charities can be found at www.jigsaw4u.org.uk. Email enquiries for Jigsaw(SouthEast) can be made to info@jigsawsoutheast.org.uk

The Family Groups create an opportunity for each family member to meet with their peers. Four to eight families are invited to the Family Groups at a time. The groups run for a period of six weeks – one weekday evening each week and one Saturday.

Adults meet with other adults. Young people meet with other young people and children meet with other children. Additionally certain activities, undertaken as a family, focus on recognising the losses they share and identifying hopes for the future.

At the Family Groups everyone engages in therapeutic activities to share memories and to explore thoughts and feelings. Meeting with peers enables each family member to feel less isolated and strong bonds are sometimes forged with other members of the group. The experience of working on identical activities provides a natural talking point for family members as they return home and this creates an awareness of each others' needs and enriches communication.

Other charities working with bereaved families

Fegans works in East Sussex, West Kent, Thanet and Lambeth to support vulnerable children and their families. Their work is a practical expression of Christian faith, embodying love, justice and forgiveness but is open to those of any faith or none. They meet a variety of emotional needs including bereavement. www. fegans.org.uk

Winston's Wish provides support to children and young people and their parents who have suffered bereavement. They offer residential weekends including specialist ones for those bereaved by murder or suicide. Their helpline is 0845 2030405. www.winstonswish.org.uk

Individual bereavement support

Cruse Bereavement Care offers one to one bereavement support for adults (usually at home) and for children (usually in school) by specially trained volunteers www.crusebereavementcare.org. uk There is an interactive website for young people www.rd4u. org.uk

My favourite books for children

5-10s

Always and Forever – Alan Durant and Debi Gliori

Badger's Parting Gifts – Susan Varley

Sad isn't Bad – Michaelene Mundy

Waterbugs and Dragonflies – Doris Stickney

What Happens when we Die? – Carolyn Nystrom

7+

Someone has Died Suddenly – Mary Williams and Steve Fraser

10+

Learning to say Good-by – Eda LeShan

Activity books

5-11s

Muddles, Puddles and Sunshine – Diana Crossley and Kate Sheppard

When Someone Very Special Dies: Children can learn to cope with grief – Marge Heegaard

8-15s

Grief Encounter – Shelley Gilbert

Games

The Grief Game – Yvonne Searle and Isabelle Streng for ages 6 to 16 and can be played as a family as a therapeutic tool and for fun!

Support and Resources for Bereaved Adults

Individual bereavement support

Cruse Bereavement Care offers one to one bereavement support for adults (usually at home) by specially trained volunteers www.crusebereavementcare.org.uk

My Favourite Books for Adults

A Grace Disguised – Jerry Sittser

Blessed be your Name – Matt and Beth Redman

Roses in December – Marilyn Willett Heavilin

Appendix B

Reflections along the Way

This is a selection of my reflections as I journeyed. Some are words as from God addressed to me. Some are my inward battles and questions and addressed to God. I include them as optional encouragement in your own pursuit of God and perhaps to inspire you to write your own reflections or poems.

Don't be Afraid

Don't be afraid,
The path I'm taking you doesn't peter out in the desert and
the darkness.
It leads to a place of beauty, of life and of gladness.
The birds are singing with joy.
The land is green and luxuriant.
A place of fruitfulness.
You'll eat and be satisfied
And you'll quench your thirst from an ever-flowing waterfall.
You'll have everything you need,
For I AM your God.
I haven't led you to die in the wilderness,
But to bring you to that land which I've promised.
Don't be afraid.

Letting Go

Yes, Father...
To know the burden isn't mine but Yours
Is all I need to know.
Yet how often do I wrestle in my mind,
Struggling with 'impossibles',
Determined apparently to wallow in my misery
And be brought lower,
Destroyed in body, thought and feeling
To become a shadow of myself in all I am and do.

Yet how I long for freedom,
A freedom from the obsession of my ever-battling mind
To find my rest in You
And know the perfect glory of Your peace,
To give You charge of all the consequences
And simply take each step
In willing submission to Your perfect way.
Father, may I know this joy.

The Fear of being Known

Father, I long for that sanctuary of deep relationship,
But I shy away from the reaching out and opening up,
Without which there can be no strong connection.
I long for there to be another way
Than to leave the dark 'security' of distance,
In which shadows conceal my blemishes,
And step into the harsh reality daylight closeness will reveal.
Yet that shadowy place of 'safety' can only be illusory,
Giving nothing and receiving nothing for fear of losing all.
In desiring to save my life I lose it.
Reality is lost.
Only the shadows remain.
And so I see but dimly
My place, my role.

Yes, Father, I know there is no other way
To move from vision to reality.
The dry bones must come together
Before You breathe in life.
Help me move with steadfastness
Towards those with whom You want me close
And allow myself to be known by them
As You know me.

Soaking

Drink in my words
Let them refresh you,
Nurture you.
Revel in my words of affirmation over you.
Let them seep deep into the very core of your being,
As oil massaging
Not just your outer skin
But deep deep within.

Breathe in my perfume.
Let it not just touch your nostrils.
Let it penetrate the very essence of yourself.
Permeating every cell.

Let the bigness of who I AM
Fill your mind.
Let it expand you.
Let it push down the barriers of your human thinking,
Then, like a surfer,
Position yourself on my waves
In the vastness of the ocean of my possibilities
And know the water is glistening
In the sunshine of my delight in you.